Building Games with Flutter

The ultimate guide to creating multiplatform games using the Flame engine in Flutter 3

Paul Teale

BIRMINGHAM—MUMBAI

Building Games with Flutter

Copyright © 2022 Packt Publishing

Every effort has been made in the preparation of this book to ensure the accuracy of the information presented. However, the information contained in this book is sold without warranty, either express or implied. Neither the author, nor Packt Publishing or its dealers and distributors, will be held liable for any damages caused or alleged to have been caused directly or indirectly by this book.

Packt Publishing has endeavored to provide trademark information about all of the companies and products mentioned in this book by the appropriate use of capitals. However, Packt Publishing cannot guarantee the accuracy of this information.

Group Product Manager: Rohit Rajkumar
Publishing Product Manager: Aaron Tanna
Senior Editor: Hayden Edwards
Content Development Editor: Rashi Dubey
Technical Editor: Saurabh Kadave
Copy Editor: Safis Editing
Project Coordinator: Rashika Ba
Proofreader: Safis Editing
Indexer: Manju Arasan
Production Designer: Aparna Bhagat
Marketing Coordinator: Anamika Singh

First published: June 2022

Production reference: 1310522

Published by Packt Publishing Ltd.
Livery Place
35 Livery Street
Birmingham
B3 2PB, UK.

ISBN 978-1-80181-698-4

www.packt.com

To my beautiful wife, Mariel, and our adorable baby boy, Alfie, who I love with all my heart. In memory of my parents, Alfred and Vera Teale.

– Paul Teale

Contributors

About the author

Paul Teale was born and raised in Leeds, West Yorkshire, before moving to London to pursue a career in software engineering. He has been a software engineer for 25+ years, covering backend, web, and mobile, where he has spent the last 13 years as a mobile developer covering Android and, more recently, Flutter. He has worked on many large projects during his career for companies including Discovery, Sky, Shazam, Visa, NBC, and Channel 5. He is a massive sci-fi fan and loves watching all the latest movies. He has been happily married to Mariel for the last 16 years and they live together in West London with their son, Alfie, and their 2 cats.

I would like to thank the people who are close to me and have supported me, especially my sisters, Sandra, Angela, and Debra.

And to my great friends, Philip Hartley, Iain Baker, and Linda Chan, who have helped me through so much in my life.

About the reviewers

Linda Chan is a software engineer with a passion for exploring new technologies, teaching children to code, and developing fun games.

Working in London for start-ups and large companies, Linda began her career as a web developer and quickly transitioned to building native iOS apps. She saw huge potential in the early days of Flutter and has not looked back.

She now resides in Wales with her husband, daughter, and cat named Qwerty. Outside of coding, Linda enjoys drawing, playing the venova, guitar, piano and searching for Koroks in the land of Hyrule.

Samarth Agarwal is an experienced software engineer who specializes in the creation of mobile and web applications. He has been an active Flutter developer and has contributed numerous text and video-based courses on app development across a wide range of technologies. As a result of his content being used on multiple platforms, Samarth has helped over 20,000 students worldwide.

Currently, Samarth is a senior software engineer at QuillBot. When he is not working, he enjoys listening to music and playing first-person shooter games, not to mention that he enjoys exploring new locations and capturing everything through a lens.

Satyam Sharma is a Flutter developer from India. He has designed, developed, and shipped several apps on the Play Store.

He enjoys playing RPGs, reading books, and traveling in his free time. If he isn't busy with that, you can almost always find him looking for new project ideas. He goes by the username `satyamx64` on the internet.

Table of Contents

3
Building a Game Design

Part 2: Graphics and Sound

4
Drawing and Animating Graphics

5
Moving the Graphics with Input

6
Playing Sound Effects and Music

7
Designing Your Own Levels

8
Scaling the Game for Web and Desktop

Part 3: Advanced Games Programming

9
Implementing Advanced Graphics Effects

10

Making Intelligent Enemies with AI

11

Finishing the Game

Appendix: Answers

Index

Other Books You May Enjoy

Preface

With its powerful tools and quick implementation capabilities, Flutter provides a new way to build scalable cross-platform apps. In this book, you'll learn how to build on your knowledge and use Flutter as the foundation for creating games.

This game development book takes a hands-on approach to building a complete game from scratch. You'll see how to get started with the Flame library and build a simple animated example to test Flame. You'll then discover how to organize and load images and audio in your Flutter game. As you advance, you'll gain insights into the game loop and set it up for fast and efficient processing. The book also guides you in using Tiled to create maps, add sprites to the maps that the player can interact with, and see how to use tilemap collision to create paths for a player to walk on. Finally, you'll learn how to make enemies more intelligent with **artificial intelligence (AI)**.

By the end of the book, you'll have gained the confidence to build fun multiplatform games with Flutter.

Who this book is for

If you are a Flutter developer looking to apply your Flutter programming skills to games development, this book is for you. Basic knowledge of Dart will assist with understanding the concepts covered.

What this book covers

Chapter 1, Getting Started with Flutter Games, explains why to use Flutter/Dart for game programming. You'll see why Flutter and Dart allow the rapid development of cross-platform games and cover the key concepts involved in game programming.

Chapter 2, Working with the Flame Engine, provides an overview of the Flame engine used throughout the book to build games.

Chapter 3, *Building a Game Design*, introduces the game we will be building, along with the game's design. The game we will build throughout the book is Gold Rush, and we'll see how to plan the content and screens for the game to build a game plan.

Chapter 4, *Drawing and Animating Graphics*, gives you a detailed look at how to draw and animate graphics on the screen. You will see what sprites are and how we move them around the screen, learn how to animate sprites for realism, and see how to detect when sprites bump into other sprites on the screen.

Chapter 5, *Moving the Graphics with Input*, provides a detailed look at how to move graphics with touch events and onscreen buttons. By drawing an onscreen joystick, we show how to move a sprite around the screen in response to the user's control of the joystick and see how to use touchscreens to move sprites.

Chapter 6, *Playing Sound Effects and Music*, gives you a detailed look at playing music and sounds in response to game events.

Chapter 7, *Designing Your Own Levels*, explains how to create game levels and navigate around them.

Chapter 8, *Scaling the Game for Web and Desktop*, details how to get the same game working across different platforms by scaling up the graphics for different screen resolutions and how navigation could differ between a computer and a phone due to the lack of physical keys on a phone.

Chapter 9, *Implementing Advanced Graphics Effects*, explains how to enhance your game graphics with powerful particle and layer effects.

Chapter 10, *Making Intelligent Enemies with AI*, covers adding intelligence to games with AI. You will see how using AI allows us to make enemies appear more intelligent by chasing our player when they are close, and how we can make our player avoid obstacles while navigating the map.

Chapter 11, *Finishing the Game*, shows you how to add extra screens to your game and navigate between them. It also explains what else you could learn and where to go for help.

To get the most out of this book

You will be expected to have some knowledge of Flutter and Dart but no knowledge of game development. The book does not teach either Flutter or Dart.

It's assumed that you have a good knowledge of your development tool of choice, such as Visual Studio Code.

Software/hardware covered in the book	Operating system requirements
Flutter v3.0.0	Windows, macOS, or Linux
Flame v1.0.0	
Dart v2.17.0	

If you are using the digital version of this book, we advise you to type the code yourself or access the code from the book's GitHub repository (a link is available in the next section). Doing so will help you avoid any potential errors related to the copying and pasting of code.

The code for the book was developed with Visual Studio Code but works equally well with Android Studio and other editors.

Download the example code files

You can download the example code files for this book from GitHub at `https://github.com/PacktPublishing/Building-Games-with-Flutter`. If there's an update to the code, it will be updated in the GitHub repository.

We also have other code bundles from our rich catalog of books and videos available at `https://github.com/PacktPublishing/`. Check them out!

Download the color images

We also provide a PDF file that has color images of the screenshots and diagrams used in this book. You can download it here: `https://static.packt-cdn.com/downloads/9781801816984_ColorImages.pdf`

Conventions used

There are a number of text conventions used throughout this book.

`Code in text`: Indicates code words in text, database table names, folder names, filenames, file extensions, pathnames, dummy URLs, user input, and Twitter handles. Here is an example: "Now that you have finished updating the `pubspec.yaml` file, save the changes."

A block of code is set as follows:

```
void main() async {
  final goldRush = GoldRush();

  WidgetsFlutterBinding.ensureInitialized();
  await Flame.device.fullScreen();
  await Flame.device.setPortrait();

  runApp(
    GameWidget(game: goldRush)
  );
}
```

When we wish to draw your attention to a particular part of a code block, the relevant lines or items are set in bold:

```
cd build/web/
python3 -m http.server 8000 &
```

Any command-line input or output is written as follows:

```
flutter pub get
```

Bold: Indicates a new term, an important word, or words that you see onscreen. For instance, words in menus or dialog boxes appear in **bold**. Here is an example: "The **Game Over!!** screen will be shown when the player dies in the game and then they return to the game menu."

Tips or Important Notes
Appear like this.

Get in touch

Feedback from our readers is always welcome.

General feedback: If you have questions about any aspect of this book, email us at customercare@packtpub.com and mention the book title in the subject of your message.

Errata: Although we have taken every care to ensure the accuracy of our content, mistakes do happen. If you have found a mistake in this book, we would be grateful if you would report this to us. Please visit www.packtpub.com/support/errata and fill in the form.

Piracy: If you come across any illegal copies of our works in any form on the internet, we would be grateful if you would provide us with the location address or website name. Please contact us at copyright@packt.com with a link to the material.

If you are interested in becoming an author: If there is a topic that you have expertise in and you are interested in either writing or contributing to a book, please visit authors.packtpub.com.

Part 1: Game Basics

In this section, you will be introduced to Flutter and the Flame game engine and to the game we will build throughout the book by describing the design of the game.

This section contains the following chapters:

1
Getting Started with Flutter Games

Welcome to *Building Games with Flutter*!

We will show you how to use Google's **Flutter** framework to build scalable games that work across mobile and web platforms. Flutter may seem a strange choice at first for building games because there are more established frameworks for making games, such as Unity or Unreal Engine, but a lot of these tools are very complex to learn and it takes a long time to start producing games with them.

Building on your existing knowledge of Flutter and **Dart**, we will take you through the steps needed to build a 2D game that will work across all supported platforms. Starting with the basics, we will build on this knowledge and gradually get on to more advanced game topics. By the end of the book, you will be able to make your own 2D games containing the following:

- Animating graphics around the screen
- Playing sound effects and music
- Controlling your player with keys, joystick, or gestures
- Detecting when graphics collide

- Creating game level maps and navigating around them
- Designing games
- Scaling the game across different platforms
- Advanced graphical effects
- Intelligent enemies

We will cover the core concepts with examples and then build on this, chapter by chapter, gradually building up a full game that works across different devices. Each chapter will contain code samples to help learn the building blocks of game development, along with the code, image, and sound resources to build our complete game. The game involves the player navigating around a map and avoiding the enemies while collecting as much gold as they can.

In this chapter, we want to delve a bit deeper into Flutter and Dart and what features they have that make them a great choice for game development. This will give you an understanding of why Flutter and Dart can be used for fast, smooth games across many platforms.

In this chapter, we will cover the following topics:

- Working with Flutter
- Using Dart
- Summarizing the book
- Creating a simple example animation

We have a lot to cover, so let's get started!

Technical requirements

In this chapter, you should have your code editor set up along with the latest versions of Flutter and Dart installed. The book is based on Flutter *v3.0.0*, Dart *2.17.0*, and Flame *v1.0.0*.

All the source code for this book can be downloaded from the Git repository at `https://github.com/PacktPublishing/Building-Games-with-Flutter.git`.

The source code for this chapter specifically can be found here: `https://github.com/PacktPublishing/Building-Games-with-Flutter/tree/main/chapter01`.

Working with Flutter

You will have used Flutter to build apps or websites before and may be wondering whether Flutter is good enough to make great games. Flutter is a great choice for game programming for the following reasons:

- Flutter has very fast rendering times and is scalable across many platforms.

- Flutter games aim to draw at 60 **frames per second** (**FPS**) for smooth animation, or 120 FPS on devices capable of supporting higher refresh rates.

- Flutter code uses a single code base to make maintenance easier and enables the code to run on many devices.

- The Flutter core is written in C++, which makes games run at native speeds.

- Flutter is cost-effective due to being open source (businesses like Flutter because they don't have to pay for expensive licenses as they have to with some other frameworks).

Unlike other frameworks, Flutter does not use native components and instead draws its own, all drawn with the lightning-fast **Skia Graphics Engine**. Skia is an open source graphics library that works on a variety of hardware and software platforms, which abstracts away platform-specific graphics APIs that are different on each platform. The APIs provide functionality for drawing shapes, text, and images.

Now that we have explained Flutter, let's delve deeper into the language that Flutter uses, Dart.

Using Dart

In this section, we will discuss Dart and the language features that make it a great fit for game development. We will discuss how Dart is compiled, and how it uses threads and garbage collection. We will also discuss great features such as how hot reload aids us in developing code fast.

Compilation types

Computer programming languages can be either static or dynamic. A static language will be compiled into machine code before it runs, such as C++. A dynamic language is executed by an interpreter, so it does not need to be compiled before running (such as JavaScript).

As programming languages evolved, virtual machines were invented, which made it easier to port a language to a new hardware platform. The code is converted to bytecode, which is then run on the virtual machine. Java is an example of a language that uses bytecode.

The virtual machine imitates hardware in software and can be ported to run on different hardware platforms, making the code portable.

As compiler technology evolved, **just-in-time** (**JIT**) compilers were invented, which improved the performance of code running on virtual machines by compiling the code on the fly.

Compiling a program into machine code before running became known as **ahead-of-time** (**AOT**) compilation. Dart is unique in that it supports both JIT and AOT compilation types, which provides a massive advantage for developers. Developers can distribute the app compiled with AOT for maximum speed and performance, which helps games run smoothly.

When running in JIT compilation mode, Flutter and Dart have an amazing feature called **stateful hot reload** that cuts down development time.

Hot reload

Flutter uses the JIT compiler to allow you to reload and run code in less than a second. This allows you to change code and see the changes reflected on the emulator or web browser instantly, while retaining the internal state of the game.

This is great for game development as you can modify code and see the effect of the change, which speeds up development massively. It feels like painting with code!

For instance, you might reposition a graphic by a few pixels or change a color. In traditional development, you would have to rebuild the code (which could take many minutes) to see the change, but in Flutter, this is instant.

Native bridge

Dynamic languages such as JavaScript communicate with the native code on the platform over a bridge, which is very slow. They do this for things such as drawing the native components of the platform they are running on.

The **native bridge** is used to provide an interface between dynamic code and native code for all code, sending state information for **user interface** (**UI**) components.

In Flutter, instead of this, Skia draws all the components on a canvas (and makes them look and feel like native components), so it bypasses the need for a native bridge.

This is massive because with a native bridge you also need to pass the state of the UI components before they can be drawn, which slows everything down and can cause your UI to skip frames instead of keeping the animation smooth.

Garbage collection

Dart uses an advanced garbage collection system that quickly handles short-lived objects in memory.

As Flutter rebuilds the widget tree every frame, it throws away the old objects and recreates new objects. In a language such as Java, this would cause issues, but Dart is optimized to handle this very quickly.

Most languages require the use of locks to access shared memory, but Dart can perform its garbage collection most of the time without using locks. This fast garbage collection results in very smooth graphics performance, which greatly enhances our game.

Thread control

The developer has more control over code execution in Dart due to the way threads are implemented. Because Dart doesn't usually require locks for accessing shared memory, unlike most other languages, we have more control over the execution of the code.

Without locks, we avoid a type of call called a race condition, which can happen when separate threads want access to the shared resource (in this case, memory) and it can't be accessed because some other thread has locked access and the lock has to be released before other threads can access it.

In this section, we have discussed how the features of the Dart language help us to write fast games. In the next section, we will summarize what you will learn throughout the book.

Summarizing the book

In the following subsections, let's start to take a look at what each chapter will explore.

Flame

In the next chapter, *Chapter 2, Working with the Flame Engine*, we will cover the basics of how to use the Flame engine library to set up a game loop, and how to organize your assets for efficient loading.

Designing a game

It is important to plan ahead so that you have a blueprint to refer to as you progress through your game.

In *Chapter 3*, *Building a Game Design*, we will talk about how to plan and design a game using an example that I will refer to throughout the book.

Graphics

Apart from text-based games, all games have graphics. The graphics are the first thing someone will see when deciding whether to buy or play your game, so it's important for these to look nice if you want to sell your game.

In *Chapter 4*, *Drawing and Animating Graphics*, we will show you how to draw graphics on the screen, and how to animate them so they look real. We will also show you how to detect when graphics collide with each other, such as a bullet hitting an enemy, which can be used to trigger another animation, such as the enemy exploding.

Input

All games require some type of input, whether this is touching a screen, pressing a key, or moving a virtual joystick to control a player.

In *Chapter 5*, *Moving the Graphics with Input*, we will explain the many methods for controlling the character so that the input and animation are synchronized and feel smooth and responsive.

Sounds

Sound effects and music play an important part in games to enhance the experience for the player. The background music also plays an important part in any game; as you play the game, the music can change to highlight something important in the game or to change the mood of the game.

In *Chapter 6*, *Playing Sound Effects and Music*, we will discuss how to synchronize playing a sound effect in response to a game event, such as playing an explosion sound when a bullet collides with an enemy.

Level design

Most games are not played on a single screen and require careful thought about how each level is designed.

In *Chapter 7, Designing Your Own Levels*, we will explain how to load graphics, sounds, and level data that is needed for the current level, to ensure we don't run into memory or performance issues, which can be a real problem when developing games for low-end devices such as mobile phones.

We will also explain how to make a map that is larger than the physical screen, and how to navigate your player around the screen and scroll the map as the player moves around.

Cross-platform games

One of the key benefits of using Flutter and Dart is the cross-platform features it has for making the game work across multiple devices. We will discuss this topic in more detail in *Chapter 8, Scaling the Game for Web and Desktop*.

Advanced graphics effects

As we mentioned earlier, graphics are the first thing a user sees so they must look impressive.

In *Chapter 9, Implementing Advanced Graphics Effects*, we discuss advanced graphical effects and what we can do to make your game look amazing.

We will use particle effects to enhance the existing graphics and make the game really stand out.

We will also discuss how graphical layers can be used to draw graphics more efficiently when there is a lot of animation on the screen.

Game AI

Games are more fun when they are realistic, which we can achieve with **artificial intelligence (AI)**.

In *Chapter 10, Making Intelligent Enemies with AI*, we will show you how to make enemies that can move from one location to another, avoiding obstacles and enemies that can hunt you when they see you.

Finishing the game

In *Chapter 11, Finishing the Game*, we will discuss some things needed to finish off the game. This will include other screens that most games have, such as a splash screen for branding and a settings screen for game options (such as controlling the volume of the music).

We will discuss how to sell your game on app stores and how to increase sales of your game through in-app purchases.

Finally, by this point in the book, we will have taught you the basics of game programming but there is so much more you could learn. We will discuss what else you should learn if you want to make more advanced games, and where to go for help if you get stuck while making games.

Now that we have provided an overview of the chapters we will cover throughout the book, in the next section, we will go through a simple animation example to show you how easy it is to get started with game programming in Flutter.

Creating a simple example animation

Here is a code sample for you to run to show how easy it is to draw and animate a simple shape.

To run this example, follow these steps:

1. First, create a new project in the command line by running the following command:

    ```
    flutter create goldrush
    ```

2. Open the `goldrush` folder that Flutter created in your code editor, and then open the `pubspec.yaml` file.

3. Update the description to the following:

    ```
    description: Flutter game from Building Games with
    Flutter
    ```

4. Update the environment SDK to the following:

    ```
    sdk: ">=2.17.0 <3.0.0"
    ```

    This is the latest version of the SDK at the time of writing the book, and supports the latest features of Flutter and Dart.

5. Under the dependencies section, we need to add a library called `Flame` (which we will talk more about in the next chapter):

    ```
    cupertino_icons: ^1.0.2
    flame: 1.0.0
    ```

    Flame is a great library and provides us with a lot of functionality needed to build games using Flutter and Dart.

6. Now that we have finished updating the pubspec.yaml file, save the changes.

7. After saving the changes, your code editor should download the new dependency. If this doesn't update, you can manually run the following command from the command line in the same directory as your project:

```
flutter pub get
```

8. Next, open the lib/main.dart file and delete all the boilerplate code.

9. Then, we need to set up the imports we will need for this example:

```
import 'dart:ui';
import 'package:flame/flame.dart';
import 'package:flame/palette.dart';
import 'package:flutter/material.dart';
import 'package:flame/game.dart';
```

10. Under this, we need to add our main function to initialize the game and the screen:

```
void main() async {
  final goldRush = GoldRush();

  WidgetsFlutterBinding.ensureInitialized();
  await Flame.device.fullScreen();
  await Flame.device.setPortrait();

  runApp(
    GameWidget(game: goldRush)
  );
}
```

Here, we set up our GoldRush game object (which we will define next) and told Flame that we want to run the game in full screen and in portrait mode. We also ran the app, passing the GameWidget.

11. Next, let's set up the game widget and some variables that we will use in the game:

```
class GoldRush with Loadable, Game {

  static const int squareSpeed = 250;
  static final squarePaint =
    BasicPalette.green.paint();
```

```
static final squareWidth = 100.0, squareHeight =
  100.0;
late Rect squarePos;

int squareDirection = 1;
late double screenWidth, screenHeight, centerX,
  centerY;
```

Let's break down what we did here:

- Here, we set up the animation speed of the square to be 250; you can adjust this to a higher number to make the animation faster or lower to make the animation slower.

- We set the color of our box to green.

- The width and height of the box are set to a fixed size of 100 pixels.

- Because we will adjust the position of the box, we use Rect for the square position, which will be initialized in onLoad once we have calculated the center of the screen for the starting position.

- We set the direction to be a positive value, which will increase the x value and move the box to the right.

- Finally, we set up the variables for the screen width and height, and the center of the screen.

12. In the onLoad function, we will calculate the center starting position of the box based on the screen size:

```
@override
Future<void> onLoad() async {
  super.onLoad();
  screenWidth =
    MediaQueryData.fromWindow(window).size.width;
  screenHeight =
    MediaQueryData.fromWindow(window).size.height;
  centerX = (screenWidth / 2) - (squareWidth / 2);
  centerY = (screenHeight / 2) - (squareHeight / 2);
  squarePos = Rect.fromLTWH(centerX, centerY,
    squareWidth, squareHeight);
}
```

13. Next, we will define the render function, which draws the square on the screen at its current position:

```
@override
void render(Canvas canvas) {
  canvas.drawRect(squarePos, squarePaint);
}
```

14. Next, we update the square position every frame based on its speed and direction, plus the time that has elapsed since the previous frame.

    Then, if the position of the square has reached the edge of the screen, we can flip the direction of the square:

```
@override
void update(double deltaTime) {
  squarePos = squarePos.translate(squareSpeed *
    squareDirection * deltaTime, 0);
  if (squareDirection == 1 && squarePos.right >
  screenWidth) {
    squareDirection = -1;
  } else if (squareDirection == -1 && squarePos.left
    < 0) {
    squareDirection = 1;
  }
}
```

15. Now, we can run the example and see our simple green square animating from left to right, reversing its direction when it hits the side of the screen.

Now, we have gone through a simple animation example to show how easy it is to get started and to give you a feel for game programming with Flutter.

Feel free to play with the code, maybe changing the color of the square or adding more squares at a different position. In the next chapter, we will dig deeper into this code.

Summary

In this chapter, we explained why Flutter and Dart are well suited to multiplatform game development. We explained the building blocks of games that we will focus on in each section of the book. Finally, we showed you a simple code example to play with.

In the next chapter, we will start using Flame, the game engine library that works with Flutter to add features related to game programming.

Questions

1. What is the minimum constant frame rate that Flutter draws at?

2. What is the name of the graphics engine used by Flutter?

3. Which platforms can we support with Flutter?

4. What is Skia and what is it used for?

5. What types of compilation does Dart support and why are they beneficial?

6. Why is stateful hot reload beneficial for rapid game development?

7. Why is Dart's garbage collection beneficial for the smooth animation used in games?

2

Working with the Flame Engine

Flame is a game engine that is added, as a library, to your Flutter project. It provides us with modules that allow us to build our game. These include support for images and sprites, animations, audio, collision detection, and more advanced modules for 2D physics and tile maps.

In this chapter, we will focus on how to get started with Flame and gain an understanding of the basics of the game engine, including its assets, game loops, and components. It's important to know all of this so that you have a good understanding of the library and how everything fits together to make games with Flame.

Once you are familiar with the basics of Flame, you will be able to progress to the more advanced topics later in the book.

In this chapter, we will cover the following topics:

- Organizing the assets in your game
- Adding the game loop
- Working with components

Technical requirements

To examine the sources mentioned in this chapter, you can download them at `https://github.com/PacktPublishing/Building-Games-with-Flutter/tree/main/chapter02`.

The Flame project is evolving very quickly, so please refer to the very latest documentation for any changes or new features at `https://flame-engine.org/docs/#/`. At the time of writing, the latest version is 1.0.0, which has been integrated with Flutter v3.0.0 onward.

To install the latest version to your project, please add the following to your `pubspec.yaml` file:

```
dependencies:
  flame: 1.0.0
```

After saving the file, the dependency will be downloaded, and the Flame modules will become available. If you followed the example at the end of the previous chapter, then you will already have this set up, so please ensure you have already done this.

The newest versions of Flame can always be found in the `pub` repository at `https://pub.dev/packages/flame/install`.

Organizing the assets in your game

Your game will include many assets, such as images, audio, fonts, maps, and game data.

As with Flutter, Flame supports the asynchronous loading of assets and caching. However, it also builds on top of that functionality to add features that are useful for images and audio, to help use and manage those assets effectively. For example, if you have a sprite sheet containing many frames of animation, you can load them and split them into their individual sprites very easily. This is covered, in more depth, in *Chapter 4, Drawing and Animating Graphics*.

All of your assets go under the `assets` folder in Flutter. I recommend the following folder structure to keep everything well organized:

```
assets
--- audio
------ music
--------- music_menu.mp3
------ sounds
```

```
--------- sound_shoot.mp3
--- images
------ sprites
--------- sprite_player.png
--------- sprite_enemy.png
--- fonts
------ font_highscore.ttf
--- maps
------ map_level.tmx
```

If they are stored within the assets folder, Flutter and Flame allow you to organize your assets however you want.

In your pubspec.yaml file, the previous assets should then look like this:

```
flutter:
  assets:
    - assets/audio/music/music_menu.mp3
    - assets/audio/sound/sound_shoot.mp3
    - assets/images/sprites/player.png
    - assets/images/sprites/enemy.png
    - assets/fonts/font_highscore.ttf
    - assets/maps/map_level.tmx
```

I recommend prefixing the asset type to make it very clear what the asset is. For instance, you might have a player sound and a player sprite, so having them named sound_player.mp3 and sprite_player.png makes what they represent clearer.

Additionally, you should load any game assets for your current screen or level in advance at the start of the game or level. Flame has an onLoad() function that you can use to override this, which we will discuss further in the next section.

Flame has some helper functions to load the different asset types:

```
await Flame.images.load('player.png');
await FlameAudio.audioCache.load('explosion.mp3');
```

Here, the load function loads the asset into Flutter's internal memory cache for faster access. Also, it's important to use async/await as the assets are loading asynchronously, so we need to wait until the assets have been loaded before continuing.

Now that we understand how to add assets to our game, let's talk about how Flame constantly redraws the screen based on the current game state.

Adding the game loop

The **game loop** controls any updates to the game state and then draws any graphics on the screen to reflect the current game state.

For instance, the player might move the character they are controlling to the right, which will then increase the x position of the player's sprite during the game state update. Now that the game state has changed, the player will be drawn at the new position.

In a more complex game, hundreds of enemy sprites could also be moving around. Therefore, the state of these sprites also needs to be calculated.

This continues in a loop, where anything that is currently on the screen is updated and then redrawn. Each redraw is known as a **game frame**.

The number of frames drawn per second reflects how smooth the game is. In Flutter, apps and games redraw at 60 **frames per second** (**FPS**) to allow for very smooth redrawing.

In Flame, there are two functions that we can override to control the updating of the game state and drawing:

```
void update (double deltaTime)
void render (Canvas canvas)
```

Let's look at these functions in more detail.

Update

In the update function, a parameter is passed called deltaTime, which tells us the time that has elapsed since the previous frame was drawn. We need this value to ensure our sprites run at consistent speeds across different devices. Devices run at different speeds depending on the processing power, so if we ignore the delta value and just run everything at the maximum speed the processor can run, the player might have trouble controlling their character properly as it would be too fast. By using the deltaTime parameter in our movement calculation, we can guarantee our sprites will move at the speed that we want on devices with different processor speeds, ensuring a consistent speed on all devices.

To see this in practice, let's break down the example in *Chapter 1, Getting Started with Flutter Games*, to understand what is going on:

```
static const int squareSpeed = 250;
int squareDirection = 1;
```

Here, we want to set the speed of our square to the consistent value of 250. Our direction will be set to a positive value of 1. If you increase the *x* value of a sprite by 1, it will move to the right, whereas if you reduce it by -1, it will move left. For the *y* position, increasing by 1 will move the sprite down, while decreasing it will move the sprite up.

We can keep track of the position using a Rect, which represents a rectangle containing the *x* and *y* positions, along with the width and height of the rectangle.

In the update function, we then translate the *x* position by considering the speed and current direction using the deltaTime parameter, as follows:

```
squarePos = squarePos.translate(squareSpeed *
    squareDirection * deltaTime, 0);
```

This translates the *x* value of the square position by multiplying the speed, direction, and deltaTime parameters together. The *y* value is 0, which means we are not translating the *y* value. This is because, in this example, we are not moving in the *y* direction. However, you can update them at the same time to travel diagonally if you ever need to.

Render

The render function has a Canvas object parameter, which is a blank canvas that we draw onto. The canvas class has many functions for drawing shapes and images directly onto the canvas, as follows:

```
canvas.drawRect(squarePos, squarePaint);
```

Here, we draw a rectangle on the canvas using the position of our sprite and using the color of the paint object to apply the paint styling. The paint object represents styling similar to CSS for the web by applying the styling to the square. In this example, the position is being updated manually by a fixed amount; however, in *Chapter 5, Moving the Graphics with Input*, we will go into greater detail about how to control the position based on the user's input.

In Flame, we implement the game loop by extending one of the base classes, which automatically calls our `update` and `render` functions continuously. In the first example from *Chapter 1*, *Getting Started with Flutter Games*, we used the `Game` mixin. This allowed us to override the `update` and `render` functions. This allowed us a lot of control over the process, but it can be very cumbersome once you start drawing and updating a lot of sprites. Then, when you start adding input controls and collision detection, it can quickly become difficult to maintain and keep track of everything.

Fortunately, Flame has classes to help with all this as your game grows, which we will discuss further in the next section.

Working with components

As with any growing code base, it's important to have a structure. This is so that the code is easy to maintain as we add more features to the game.

Currently, our code contains a simple example of how to render and update a square on the screen, using the `Game` mixin to override these functions.

Using the `Game` mixin gives us a lot of control over our code, but we would have to write a lot of extra code to support the game as the game grows. This is great once you become more familiar with Flame and games programming and want that level of control. However, to begin, it's better to extend from the `FlameGame` class.

Components provide us with a structured way to organize our game as our game increases in complexity.

FlameGame

The `FlameGame` class builds on the `Game` mixin and adds a lot of useful functionality to help us manage the complexity of our game as it grows. This includes the following:

- **Flame Component System**
- Collision detection tracking
- Default implementations for `render` and `update`

Flame Component System allows us to split parts of our game up into components (classes) that represent an entity in our game, such as the player. For instance, we can have a `SpriteComponent` component to encapsulate everything related to our player sprite to manage drawing and updating any objects the player has collided with, or any other state that is specifically related to the player.

The `FlameGame` class maintains a list of all components for the game, and these can be added dynamically to the game as needed; for instance, we might add several enemy `SpriteComponent` components to the game and then remove them from the game as the player kills the enemies. Then, the `FlameGame` class will iterate over these components by telling each component to update and render itself.

Flame Component System has a lot of different types of components to help with managing different parts of our game. Here is a list of some of the most common components:

- `SpriteComponent`: For managing any sprites our game has
- `JoystickComponent`: A virtual joystick for managing input
- `TextComponent`: Text that we draw on the screen, such as the score
- `ParticleComponent`: Particle graphic effects

The complete hierarchy for the component system can be seen at `https://docs.flame-engine.org/1.0.0/components.html`.

As you can see from the component diagram at the top of Flame's website, there are a lot of components in which to handle different things, but most of the interesting ones extend from `PositionComponent`.

The `PositionComponent` component represents an object on the screen that has variables to keep track of the position, the size, and the angle direction of the component.

`SpriteComponent` extends from `PositionComponent`, so it gains these variables by default because we are going to need to position and size our sprites.

It then adds extra variables that are more specific to sprites, such as the `renderFlipX` and `renderFlipY` variables, to reverse anything drawn to the canvas. This can be useful if you have an image of a character walking from left to right; by setting `renderFlipX` to `true`, it will then draw the sprite images in reverse so that it appears to be walking from right to left.

Any components that are added to the `FlameGame` class can also be tracked for collision detection once we have set up the component's bounding boxes. After setting this up, we will get a callback in an `onCollision` function that we override. This tells us which components our component has collided with. This makes something that is quite difficult to keep track of much simpler. We will discuss collision detection, in more depth, later.

Let's convert our existing code to use the `FlameGame` class and Flame Component System.

Converting our code to use components

In this section, we will convert our previous code to use components that improve the readability and maintainability of our code. To do this, perform the following steps:

1. Create a new directory under our `lib` directory to store our components, called `components`. You can do this in Visual Studio Code by right-clicking on the `lib` folder and selecting **New Folder**. Alternatively, you can do this from the command line within the `lib` directory:

    ```
    mkdir components
    ```

2. In the new `components` directory, create a new file, called `player.dart`, where we will add our new component code for the player.

3. Open the file, and let's start defining our player's `PositionComponent`. At the top of the file, import the components package from the Flame library:

    ```
    import 'dart.ui';
    import 'package:flame/components.dart';
    import 'package:flame/geometry.dart';
    import 'package:flame/palette.dart';
    import 'package:flutter/material.dart';
    ```

4. Next, we define the outline for our `Player` class by overriding the `update` and `render` functions:

    ```
    class Player extends PositionComponent {

      @override
      void update(double deltaTime) {
        super.update(deltaTime);
      }

      @override
      void render(Canvas canvas) {
        super.render(canvas);
      }
    }
    ```

5. A requirement of the overriding components is that we must call the `base` class using `super` for both the `update` and `render` functions.

    In the `update` and `render` functions, let's copy the code from our `GoldRush` game class to our `Player` class after the `super` calls to the base class:

    ```
    @override
    void update(double deltaTime) {
    super.update(deltaTime);

    squarePos = squarePos.translate(squareSpeed *
      squareDirection * deltaTime, 0);
    if (squareDirection == 1 &&
      squarePos.right > screenWidth) {
        squareDirection = -1;
        }
    else if (squareDirection == -1 &&
      squarePos.left < 0) {
          squareDirection = 1;
        }
      }

      @override
      void render(Canvas canvas) {
        super.render(canvas);

        canvas.drawRect(squarePos, squarePaint);
      }
    ```

6. In your code editor, the square variables might now be highlighted in red; this is because we haven't yet defined those variables in this class. So, to do that, let's move them from the `GoldRush` class and add the following to the top of the `Player` class:

    ```
    static const int squareSpeed = 250;
    static final squarePaint =
      BasicPalette.green.paint();
    static final squareWidth = 100.0,
      squareHeight = 100.0;
    late Rect squarePos;
    ```

```
int squareDirection = 1;
late double screenWidth, screenHeight, centerX,
  centerY;
```

7. To calculate the initial square position, the screen dimensions, and the center of the screen, let's move the onLoad function from the GoldRush class to inside our Player component, just below where we defined the variables:

```
@override
Future<void> onLoad() async {
super.onLoad();
  screenWidth =
    MediaQueryData.fromWindow(window).size.width;
  screenHeight =
    MediaQueryData.fromWindow(window).size.height;

  centerX = (screenWidth / 2) - (squareWidth / 2);
  centerY = (screenHeight / 2) - (squareHeight / 2);
  squarePos = Rect.fromLTWH(centerX, centerY,
    squareWidth, squareHeight);
}
```

8. Now, in the GoldRush class, you can remove the variables and the functions for render, update, and onLoad that have moved to the Player class.

9. Next, let's change the class definition to use the FlameGame class instead of the Game mixin:

```
class GoldRush extends FlameGame {
```

10. In the GoldRush class imports, you can tidy up any imports that are no longer required in this class for palette and the UI.

    Now we are going to add the Player component to our FlameGame class so that it can keep track of this component for drawing and updating purposes. Let's add the Player component to the GoldRush onLoad function:

```
@override
Future<void> onLoad() async {
    super.onLoad();
    add(Player());
}
```

11. Then, update the imports to add the `Player` component:

    ```
    import 'components/player.dart';
    ```

12. Now, if you run the game, you will see that everything works as before, with the green square animating from left to right and bouncing off the sides.

    Because we added the `Player` component to the `onLoad` function, the `FlameGame` class is now tracking the component and calling its own `onLoad` function to initialize the sprite. Then, it continuously calls the sprite's `update` and `render` functions to animate the square.

    As mentioned previously, another great feature of using the `FlameGame` class is the collision detection tracking for every registered component once we have initialized the component's bounding box. So, let's do that next.

13. In the `GoldRush` class, first, we add the `HasCollidables` mixin as follows:

    ```
    class GoldRush extends FlameGame with HasCollidables {
    ```

    This tells the `FlameGame` class to start tracking any collidable objects that we want to track.

14. In the `onLoad` function, we are now going to add a special type of collidable object that we want to check for, called `ScreenCollidable`. If we add `ScreenCollidable` to our list of collidable components to track, we will be notified any time our bouncing square hits the edges of the screen:

    ```
    @override
    Future<void> onLoad() async {
      super.onLoad();

      add(Player());
      add(ScreenCollidable());
    }
    ```

15. Also, let's import `package:flame/components.dart` where `ScreenCollidable` is, as follows:

    ```
    import 'package:flame/components.dart';
    ```

16. Now, in our `Player` class, in the line that defines the class, we need to add the `HasHitboxes` and `Collidable` mixins:

```
class Player extends PositionComponent with HasHitboxes,
Collidable {
```

This will allow us to receive a callback when we collide with the sides of the screen in the `onCollision` function, which we will implement next.

17. Implement the `onCollision` function by adding the following:

```
@override
void onCollision(Set<Vector2> points,
  Collidable other) {
  if (other is ScreenCollidable) {
    if (squareDirection == 1) {
      squareDirection = -1;
    } else {
      squareDirection = 1;
    }
  }
}
```

Here, when we receive a callback to `onCollision` to tell us what component we have collided with, we check whether we have collided with `ScreenCollidable`, and if so, we simply flip the direction the square is traveling in.

18. Now that we are using the built-in collision tracking system, we must set up the position of our sprite correctly for the bounding box to be set, so we will use the built-in position variable that is inherited from the `PositionComponent` component.

First, you can delete or comment the `squarePos` rectangle as we no longer need this:

```
// late Rect squarePos;
```

19. Then, in the `onLoad` function, delete or comment the following line:

```
// squarePos = Rect.fromLTWH(centerX, centerY,
//   squareWidth, squareHeight);
```

20. Below this, we will set up the internal variables, `position` and `size`:

```
position = Vector2(centerX, centerY);
size = Vector2(squareWidth, squareHeight);
```

Here, we are setting the position and size based on our existing variables where we calculate the center of the screen and have a fixed value for the width and height.

21. Next, we need to add a shape for the `HitBox` mixin or it won't detect that it has collided with anything. There are a few built-in shapes that you can use depending on the shape of your sprite and which points of the sprite you want to use for collision detection. Most commonly, your sprites will be rectangular/square-shaped, so you could use `HitBoxRectangle` as your shape. However, if your sprite were a ball, you would use `HitBoxCircle` instead. You can also make custom shapes, but in most cases, that is unnecessary.

    Our shape is a square, so let's add our shape for the collision tracking where we just set up the position and size, as follows:

```
addHitbox(HitboxRectangle());
```

22. Our `onLoad` function should now look like this:

```
@override
Future<void> onLoad() async {
  super.onLoad();
  screenWidth =
    MediaQueryData.fromWindow(window).size.width;
  screenHeight =
    MediaQueryData.fromWindow(window).size.height;
  centerX = (screenWidth / 2) - (squareWidth / 2);
  centerY = (screenHeight / 2) - (squareHeight / 2);
  position = Vector2(centerX, centerY);
  size = Vector2(squareWidth, squareHeight);
  addHitbox(HitboxRectangle());
}
```

23. Now that we have removed our `squarePos` rectangle, we need to update the `render` and `update` functions to use the internal position value:

```
@override
void render(Canvas canvas) {
  super.render(canvas);
```

```
    renderHitboxes(canvas, paint: squarePaint);
  }
```

Because we have set up a HitBox mixin that is the same shape and uses the position and size of the PositionComponent component, we can use a built-in function, called renderHitboxes, to draw our shape. Note that we pass in our squarePaint object to keep the look the same.

In the update function, we can remove a lot of code, as updating the position has now become much simpler and our direction change is already handled by the collision tracking:

```
@override
void update(double deltaTime) {
  super.update(deltaTime);
  position.x +=
    squareSpeed * squareDirection * deltaTime;
}
```

Now our code is looking better, and the Player class is taking care of updating its location and rendering, along with dealing with any collisions.

Summary

In this chapter, you were introduced to Flame, which is a great library for building games with Flutter. Additionally, you learned how to set up Flame and organize your assets. We covered the game loop and why the render and update functions are important. Finally, we covered components and converted our existing code to use components for a more organized structure as our game expands.

In the next chapter, we will discuss how to design games using the design template, which we will use for our own game: Gold Rush!

Questions

1. What does the deltaTime value that is passed to the update function represent?
2. How does Flame Component System benefit your code?
3. What shape should you use for detecting a collision with square sprites?

3
Building a Game Design

Now that we have discussed Flame and shown you some basic animation, we want to discuss the game we are going to build throughout the rest of the book.

The game will be called Gold Rush, and has the following objectives:

- Avoid being attacked by zombies and skeletons.
- Explore the map, collecting as many gold coins as you can before you die.

It will be a simple game but will teach you a lot of skills by adding a lot of common features included in most games, including the following:

- Drawing sprite graphics
- Detecting collisions between sprites
- Controlling a player with virtual joysticks, touch, or keys
- Playing music and sounds
- Drawing and moving around maps larger than the screen
- Drawing particle and shadow advanced graphical effects

- Creating intelligent enemies
- Navigating around obstacles
- Navigating between game screens

We will go through each of these topics in turn, gradually building out a full game. We will cover the following topics in this chapter:

- Planning a game
- Designing the game screens

Planning a game

Let's start by defining a synopsis for our game that we could use to market the game and give a brief reason to the player why they might want to play the game. Here is the synopsis:

In Gold Rush, you play as an explorer who must travel across the land in search of wealth by collecting any gold coins you can find. Beware, though: the path ahead won't be easy. You must avoid the zombies and skeletons that roam the land in search of your blood!

A nice, simple summary that tells the player what the goal of the game is and what they must do to succeed (collect as much gold as possible) while avoiding losing the game (by being attacked by zombies and skeletons).

In most games, you have a main character who is the game representation of yourself. In our game, this is George.

Figure 3.1 – Our protagonist, George

George will move around the game map controlled by the player either by the touch on a location on the screen, by controlling the on-screen joystick, or with the keys on a physical keyboard.

George can run to try to escape the enemies that are chasing him. His health is measured as a percentage that starts at 100% and decreases by 25% each time he is caught by a zombie or skeleton. Once George's health reaches 0, it's game over.

There are two types of enemies in the game – zombies and skeletons.

Figure 3.2 – Our game enemies, zombies and skeletons

The enemies will chase George when he is nearby and within their line of sight. When they catch George, they will explode on impact and die, reducing George's health by 25%.

George will take the risk of being killed by zombies and skeletons because he can become very rich by avoiding the enemies and collecting the gold coins that are scattered around the map.

Figure 3.3 – The gold coins George collects to become richer

Every time George collects a spinning gold coin, his score increases by 20.

George has a large game world to explore, which will scroll around the screen as he explores.

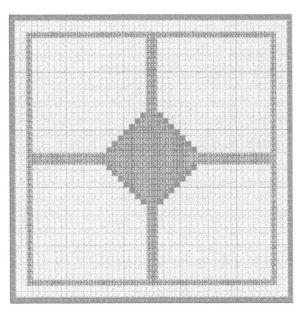

Figure 3.4 – The game world George can explore

The game world is mostly grass but has paths that George can follow. The map is surrounded by water, which George cannot cross. There is a central diamond area, which is the focal point of the map and is surrounded by water for decoration.

The game world is made up of a tile map using the **Tiled** application, which allows us to reuse smaller tiles to make larger maps efficiently. The following image is used to create our game world map (available at `https://opengameart.org`) and is originally created by *Luis Zuno*:

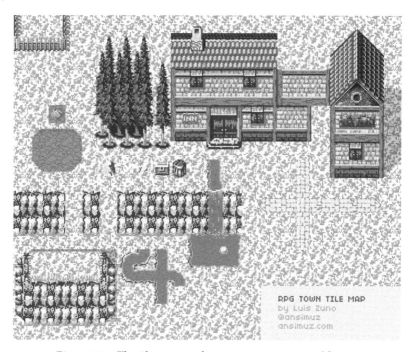

Figure 3.5 – The tile map used to create our game world map

The game will use music and sound to enhance the game. There is background music that will play while the game is playing, and the volume for this will be changeable in the game settings.

There are three sound effects that we will use during the game:

- **George movement** – A running sound that will play constantly while George is moving.

- **Enemy dying** – Every time an enemy attacks George, it will die and make this sound.

- **Coins** – Every time George collects a coin, this sound will play.

The sound will stop playing if the game is placed in the background on mobile.

Now that we have discussed our game content, let's discuss the designs of the game screens and how to navigate between them.

Designing the game screens

Now that we have discussed the elements of the game, let's discuss the screens we will use in the game and how the player will navigate between them.

The following is a basic outline to illustrate the flow of the game screens:

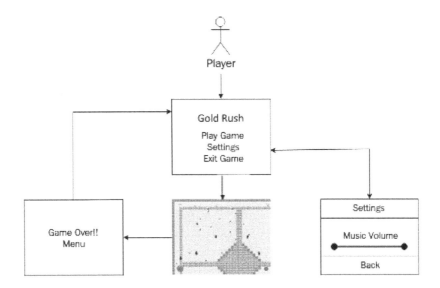

Figure 3.6 – Gold Rush screen game flow

Here, we can see the player is shown the game menu at the start, where they can play the game, go to the settings screen, or exit the game.

If they choose **Play Game**, the game is loaded and they begin to play the game.

If they choose **Settings**, they can adjust the music and then return to the game menu.

The **Game Over!!** screen will be shown when the player dies in the game and then they can return to the game menu.

Let's have a look at the final designs and appearances for these screens.

The following screenshot shows the game menu screen:

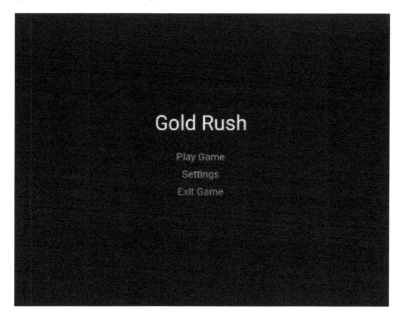

Figure 3.7 – The game menu screen for Gold Rush

This is what the **Settings** screen will look like:

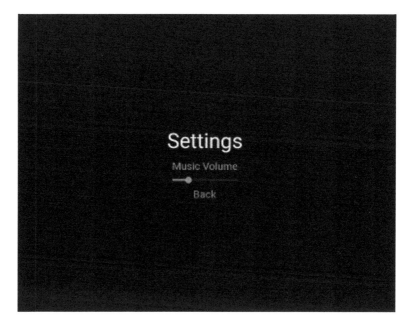

Figure 3.8 – The Settings screen for Gold Rush

Figure 3.9 shows the screen when the game is over:

Figure 3.9 – The Game Over!! screen for Gold Rush

The following screenshot shows George, the enemies, the map, and virtual controls for Gold Rush:

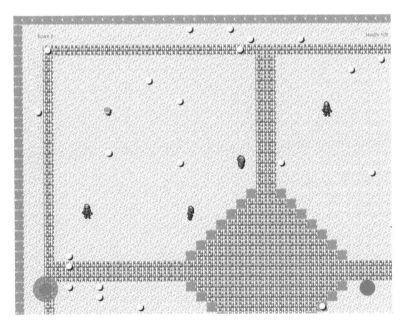

Figure 3.10 – Game screen showing George, the enemies, the map, and virtual controls

In this section, we walked through how the game screens will look and how to navigate between them.

Summary

In this chapter, we discussed the aim of the game and what the sprites and screens will look like.

When you are planning your games, try and put together a game design document like we discussed in this chapter, as it will be a useful blueprint of the game you intend to build that you can refer to during game development.

Try and think about the content that you want to add, even if you don't know how it will look yet. You can even draw stick men figures to represent the sprites if you haven't made the final decision of which sprites you will use.

In the next chapter, we will start to build out the game, starting with drawing and animating sprites.

Questions

1. Why is making a synopsis a good idea for your game?
2. How much health will George lose when an enemy attacks him?
3. How many points does George gain for collecting a gold coin?
4. What is water used for on the game map?

Part 2: Graphics and Sound

In this part of the book, we will demonstrate how to use the media capabilities of the Flame library to animate graphics and play sound. We will also discuss how to animate the graphics based on input received from the player. Finally, we will discuss level design and how to scale your game across multiple platforms.

This part contains the following chapters:

- *Chapter 4, Drawing and Animating Graphics*
- *Chapter 5, Moving the Graphics with Input*
- *Chapter 6, Playing Sound Effects and Music*
- *Chapter 7, Designing Your Own Levels*
- *Chapter 8, Scaling the Game for Web and Desktop*

4
Drawing and Animating Graphics

In this chapter, we will go beyond drawing simple shapes and discuss how to draw and animate pixel graphics seen in most games. This will make our game look much nicer and bring the game to life as the characters animate around the screen.

In game programming, a graphic or image that is drawn to the screen is known as a **sprite**, which can be anything from a single non-animated image, a player character with multiple frames of animation, or even the background image drawn behind other graphics on the screen.

We will start by showing how to load and draw a simple sprite instead of our square, and then animate the sprite to show movement. Next, we will move the sprite around the screen and the animation will change based on the direction the sprite is currently moving in.

And finally, we will create an enemy sprite for the player sprite to collide into as we build on our knowledge of collision detection.

So, we will cover the following topics:

- Drawing on the screen
- Working with sprite animation
- Moving a sprite around the screen
- Colliding with other sprites

Let's get started by setting up the assets we will use for this chapter.

Technical requirements

To examine the source from this chapter, you can download it from `https://github.com/PacktPublishing/Building-Games-with-Flutter/tree/main/chapter04`.

For this chapter, you will also need to download some images to use for the animation.

Also, I used the sprite sheets downloadable from the following links:

- For our player character, we will use the sprite sheet image at `https://github.com/PacktPublishing/Building-Games-with-Flutter/blob/main/chapter04/assets/images/george.png`.
- For the enemies, we will use the sprite sheet image at `https://github.com/PacktPublishing/Building-Games-with-Flutter/blob/main/chapter04/assets/images/zombie_n_skeleton.png`.

Now, we will add the images to our game with the following steps:

1. Open your file manager and go to the `goldrush` folder for your project.
2. Create a folder called `assets` in the `goldrush` folder.
3. Go into the `assets` folder and create another folder called `images`.
4. Move the two images we downloaded into the `images` folder.

   If you have set up everything correctly, your directory structure will look like this:

   ```
   goldrush
   --- assets
   ------ images
   --------- george.png
   --------- zombie_n_skeleton.png
   ```

5. Next, open the `pubspec.yaml` file located in the project folder.

6. Uncomment the `assets` line by removing the # symbol at the beginning of this line:

```
# assets:
```

7. Next, add the following lines below the `asset` line (notice the missing #):

```
assets:
    - assets/images/george.png
    - assets/images/zombie_n_skeleton.png
```

8. If you now save the `pubspec.yaml` file, it will check for changes in the file to confirm that it is set up correctly. If this doesn't happen, you can manually run the following from a terminal:

```
flutter pub get
```

In this section, we downloaded and set up the sprites we will use during this chapter.

In the next section, we will see how to load the sprite sheets containing multiple animation frames and draw the sprite on the screen.

Drawing on the screen

Now that we are familiar with drawing basic shapes on the screen, which we covered in the previous chapter, we will expand our knowledge and start drawing sprites, which are more common in games.

Let's create a new `SpriteComponent` for our character, George, and load the sprite sheet:

1. In the `components` folder, create a new file called `george.dart`.

2. Open the file and add the following imports at the top of the file:

```
import 'package:flame/components.dart';
import 'package:flame/flame.dart';
import 'package:flame/sprite.dart';
import 'package:flutter/material.dart';
import 'dart:ui';
```

3. Create a class called George, which extends `SpriteComponent`:

    ```
    class George extends SpriteComponent {
    }
    ```

4. At the top of the class, let's define some variables for the sprite, screen dimensions, and sprite size:

    ```
    late double screenWidth, screenHeight, centerX, centerY;
    late double georgeSizeWidth = 48.0, georgeSizeHeight =
    48.0;
    ```

    As the sprite sheet size is 192 x 192 pixels with four rows and columns, this means that each individual frame is *192 / 4 = 48* pixels width and height, which is what we have set the values of `georgeSizeWidth` and `georgeSizeHeight` to.

5. Next, we will override the `onLoad` function, set up the screen variables, load the sprite sheet, and set up our sprite's position and size:

    ```
    @override
    Future<void> onLoad() async {
      super.onLoad();
      screenWidth =
        MediaQueryData.fromWindow(window).size.width;
      screenHeight =
        MediaQueryData.fromWindow(window).size.height;

      centerX =
        (screenWidth / 2) - (georgeSizeWidth / 2);
      centerY =
        (screenHeight / 2) - (georgeSizeHeight / 2);

      var spriteImages =
        await Flame.images.load('george.png');
      final spriteSheet = SpriteSheet(image:
        spriteImages, srcSize: Vector2(georgeSizeWidth,
          georgeSizeHeight));
    ```

```
    sprite = spriteSheet.getSprite(0, 0);

    position = Vector2(centerX, centerY);
    size = Vector2(georgeSizeWidth, georgeSizeHeight);
}
```

Here, we use the Flame helper class to load the sprite sheet images and set up the sprite.

For now, we are going to get the first sprite frame and show only that frame. The first frame we get is *0, 0* in the sprite sheet:

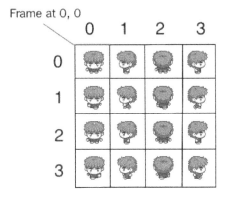

Figure 4.1 – Sprite at 0, 0

6. Now, let's switch to the main.dart file, so we can add the George component to see it on the screen. In the onLoad function, we can remove the lines that add the Player and ScreenCollidable components, and add the George component, like this:

```
@override
Future<void> onLoad() async {
    super.onLoad();
    add(George());
}
```

7. We can now remove the following imports of the Player and ScreenCollidable components that were used to show the green square, which we used in *Chapter 2, Working with the Flame Engine*:

```
import 'components/player.dart';
import 'package:flame/comonents.dart';
```

8. And, as we are no longer using the `Player` component, we can also delete the `player.dart` file containing the `Player` component, which is not needed anymore.

9. As we have added the `George` component, we need to add the import for the class at the top of the file with other imports:

    ```
    import 'package:goldrush/components/george.dart';
    ```

    If you run the game now, you will see a single frame showing George on a black background.

    It's difficult to see against the black background though, so let's create a `Background` component and change the background color, which will be drawn before George, so we can see the sprite more clearly.

10. In the `components` folder, create a new file called `background.dart`. Open the file and enter the following imports and code:

    ```
    import 'package:flame/components.dart';
    import 'package:flame/palette.dart';
    import 'package:flutter/material.dart';
    import 'dart:ui';

    class Background extends PositionComponent {

      static final backgroundPaint =
        BasicPalette.white.paint();
      late double screenWidth, screenHeight;

      @override
      Future<void> onLoad() async {
        super.onLoad();
        screenWidth =
          MediaQueryData.fromWindow(window).size.width;
        screenHeight =
          MediaQueryData.fromWindow(window).size.height;
    ```

```
    position = Vector2(0, 0);
    size = Vector2(screenWidth, screenHeight);
  }


  @override
  void render(Canvas canvas) {
    super.render(canvas);

canvas.drawRect(Rect.fromPoints(position.toOffset(),
  size.toOffset()), backgroundPaint);
    }
  }
```

In the onLoad function, we set backgroundPaint to white to make the George sprite more visible. We also set the position to 0, 0, and the size to the full width and height of the screen, so that when we paint the white color in the render function, it covers the whole screen.

11. Back in the main.dart file, let's add import to the top of the file and the Background component to the onLoad function:

```
import 'components/background.dart';
  @override
  Future<void> onLoad() async {
    super.onLoad();
    add(Background());
    add(George());
  }
```

Note that we add the Background component before the George component so that it gets drawn first.

If you run this, you will now see George drawn against a white background, which is much easier to see:

Figure 4.2 – George on a white background

In the next section, we will discuss how to animate George instead of just showing a single frame.

Working with sprite animation

Let's change the `George` class to play an animation sequence instead of just a single frame by changing the class:

1. First, change the class definition to extend from `SpriteAnimationComponent` instead of `SpriteComponent`:

    ```
    class George extends SpriteAnimationComponent {
    ```

2. Because we are going to set up an animation within `SpriteAnimationComponent`, we can remove the references to `georgeSprite` as this will be managed by the class. So, let's remove or comment the following lines:

    ```
    // late Sprite georgeSprite;


    // georgeSprite = spriteSheet.getSprite(0, 0);
    ```

    You can also remove or comment the `render` function now as the drawing will be managed by the class:

    ```
    // @override
    // void render(Canvas canvas) {
    //   super.render(canvas);

    //   georgeSprite.render(canvas);
    // }
    ```

3. To create an animation from the sprite sheet we set up, the `SpriteSheet` class has a `createAnimation` helper function, which allows us to set which row the animation should be created from. If you look closely at our `george.png` file, you will notice that our animations are in columns and not rows. At the time of writing, the current version of the Flame `createAnimation` library works with rows and not columns, so we will use Dart extensions to add a variant of `createAnimation` to the `SpriteSheet` class that works on columns too. After the class definition for our `SpriteAnimationComponent` in `george.dart`, add the following:

    ```
    extension CreateAnimationByColumn on SpriteSheet {
        SpriteAnimation createAnimationByColumn({
          required int column,
          required double stepTime,
          bool loop = true,
    ```

```
        int from = 0,
        int? to,
      }) {
      to ??= columns;
      final spriteList = List<int>.generate(to - from,
        (i) => from + i)
          .map((e) => getSprite(e, column))
          .toList();

      return SpriteAnimation.spriteList(
        spriteList,
        stepTime: stepTime,
        loop: loop,
      );
    }
  }
```

This extension will create a list of sprites based on the column and then create a `SpriteAnimation` from the sprite list.

4. Now, we can use the sprite list to create an animation that we will assign to our `SpriteAnimationComponent` animation field. At the end of the `onLoad` function, add the following code:

```
animation = spriteSheet.createAnimationByColumn(
  column: 0, stepTime: 0.2);
```

Here, we call the new `createAnimationByColumn` extension function, passing 0 for the first column animation, and the `stepTime` animation speed to 0.2, which gives the impression of a normal walking speed in the animation.

Now, we have expanded our sprite by drawing multiple frames to create an animation.

In the next section, we will set up animations for each of George's directions and move him around the screen, changing directions every few seconds, and changing the animation to match the direction he is traveling in.

Moving a sprite around the screen

Now that we have the George sprite animating, we will build on that and change the animation based on the direction of travel:

1. Let's add some variables at the top of the George class to store the animations and direction information:

    ```
    late SpriteAnimation georgeDownAnimation,
      georgeLeftAnimation, georgeUpAnimation,
      georgeRightAnimation;
    double elapsedTime = 0.0;
    double georgeSpeed = 40.0;
    int currentDirection = down;
    static const int down = 0, left = 1, up = 2,
      right = 3;
    ```

2. Below the onLoad function, define a new function called changeDirection, which we will call every 3 seconds to change George's direction randomly:

    ```
    void changeDirection() {
      Random random = Random();
      int newDirection = random.nextInt(4);

      switch (newDirection) {
        case down:
          animation = georgeDownAnimation;
          break;
        case left:
          animation = georgeLeftAnimation;
          break;
        case up:
          animation = georgeUpAnimation;
          break;
        case right:
          animation = georgeRightAnimation;
          break;
      }
    ```

```
            currentDirection = newDirection;
        }
```

Here, we generate a random number between 0 and 3 that maps to our columns. Then, we set the `animation` class field to use the animations, which we will initialize shortly. Finally, we set the current direction to be the new direction, which we can use to move the sprite later.

3. At the bottom of the `onLoad` function, remove the line that sets up the class field animation, as we now do this in the `changeDirection` function, and replace it with the following lines to initialize the animations:

```
        georgeDownAnimation =
          spriteSheet.createAnimationByColumn(column: 0,
            stepTime: 0.2);
        georgeLeftAnimation =
          spriteSheet.createAnimationByColumn(column: 1,
            stepTime: 0.2);
        georgeUpAnimation =
          spriteSheet.createAnimationByColumn(column: 2,
            stepTime: 0.2);
        georgeRightAnimation =
          spriteSheet.createAnimationByColumn(column: 3,
            stepTime: 0.2);

        changeDirection();
```

4. Now we have our animations set up, let's add an `update` function to change direction every 3 seconds and move the sprite in the same direction that the animation is facing. Under the `changeDirection` function, add the following `update` function code:

```
        @override
        void update(double deltaTime) {
          super.update(deltaTime);

          elapsedTime += deltaTime;
          if (elapsedTime > 3.0) {
```

```
      changeDirection();
      elapsedTime = 0.0;
    }

    switch (currentDirection) {
      case down:
        position.y += georgeSpeed * deltaTime;
        break;
      case left:
        position.x -= georgeSpeed * deltaTime;
        break;
      case up:
        position.y -= georgeSpeed * deltaTime;
        break;
      case right:
        position.x += georgeSpeed * deltaTime;
        break;
    }
  }
```

5. Finally, let's fix the import for the `Random` class by adding the following line at the top of this file:

```
import 'dart:math';
```

If you run the code now, you will see George move around for 3 seconds and then change direction randomly, occasionally continuing in the same direction if the random number chosen is the same as the previous 3 seconds. If you let this run for a while, you may see George vanish off the side of the screen, as we currently aren't detecting when he collides with the edge of the screen.

In the next section, we will make George flip direction when he collides with the edge of the screen, and add zombies and skeletons that move around and die if George collides with them.

Colliding with other sprites

Let's fix the issue with George wandering off the edge of the screen that we saw at the end of the last section and flip the direction if he hits the edge of the screen. To do this, follow these steps:

1. In the onLoad function of main.dart, let's add the ScreenCollidable component to the bottom of the function so we can detect collisions between George and the screen edges:

    ```
    add(ScreenCollidable());
    ```

2. In the george.dart file, change the class definition to add the HasHitBoxes and Collidable mixins:

    ```
    class George extends SpriteAnimationComponent with
    HasHitBoxes, Collidable {
    ```

3. At the bottom of the onLoad function, add the HitboxRectangle shape for the collision detection:

    ```
    addHitbox(HitboxRectangle());
    ```

4. Add the following import at the top of the file to resolve the reference to HitboxRectangle:

    ```
    import 'package:flame/geometry.dart';
    ```

5. At the bottom of this class file, after the update function definition, add the following onCollision function definition:

    ```
    @override
    void onCollision(Set<Vector2> points,
      Collidable other) {
      if (other is ScreenCollidable) {
        switch (currentDirection) {
          case down:
            currentDirection = up;
            animation = georgeUpAnimation;
            break;
          case left:
            currentDirection = right;
            animation = georgeRightAnimation;
    ```

```
          break;
        case up:
          currentDirection = down;
          animation = georgeDownAnimation;
          break;
        case right:
          currentDirection = left;
          animation = georgeLeftAnimation;
          break;
      }

      elapsedTime = 0.0;
    }
  }
```

Here, we flip the `currentDirection` and animation if George collides with the edge of the screen; for instance, if George was moving right, he will now move left, and the animation will change to `georgeLeftAnimation`. We also reset `elapsedTime` to `0.0` so that our 3-second counter starts again.

If you run the game now, you will see that after some time, when George hits the side of the screen, he will flip direction and the animation will update. You can change the `georgeSpeed` variable value to speed this up if you like.

Next, let's add the zombies and skeletons to the game!

If you look at the sprite sheet for the zombies and skeletons, you will notice both are in the same sprite sheet, both are organized by rows and now columns, and both have a zombie and a skeleton on each row. So, while we are building the animations, we must specify a `from` and `to` field to indicate which part of the sprite sheet makes up the animation.

For example, for the animation that makes the zombie's direction walk to the left, it would be on row `1`, from column `0` to `2`. The sprite image is 192 pixels wide by 256 pixels high containing six frames horizontally and four frames down, so to calculate the size of a sprite, it would be as follows:

```
192 / 6 = 32
256 / 4 = 64
```

So, our sprite size is 32 pixels in width and 64 pixels high:

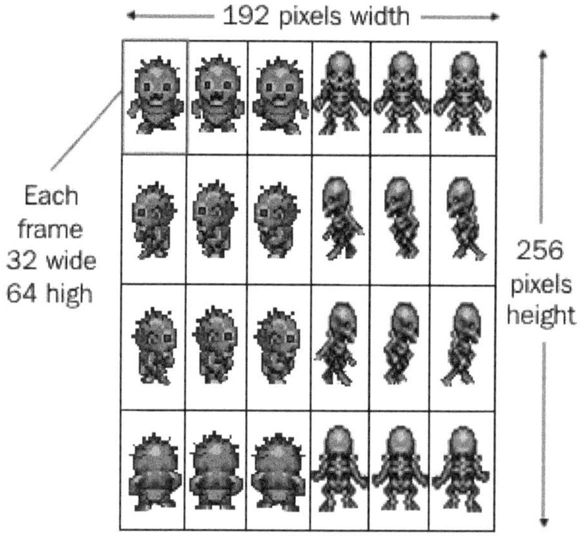

Figure 4.3 – Enemy sprites, showing the size of each frame

If we make a class for our zombie and skeleton, the code would be very similar to the George class because we need to load the sprites, organize them into animations, update the animations based on directions, and flip the direction if we bump into the edge of the screen.

To avoid a lot of unnecessary code duplication, we are going to create a base class for all our sprites for this common functionality. Then, the individual classes will be much smaller to keep the code clean and easy to read.

To start with, we will move a lot of the code from the George class into a new base class we will call Character. As we do this, we will make the variable names more generic, such as renaming georgeSpeed to speed and adding a constructor to pass values such as the position, size, and speed to make this more flexible.

6.   In the components folder, create a new file called character.dart with the following class definition:

```
import 'dart:math';
import 'package:flame/components.dart';
import 'package:flame/sprite.dart';
```

```
class Character extends SpriteAnimationComponent with
    HasHitboxes, Collidable {
}
```

7. Next, we add a constructor for passing the position, size, and speed and some variables for the animations and direction information:

```
Character({required Vector2 position,
    required Vector2 size, required double speed}) {
        this.position = position;
        this.size = size;
        this.speed = speed;
}

late SpriteAnimation downAnimation, leftAnimation,
    upAnimation, rightAnimation;
late double speed;
double elapsedTime = 0.0;
int currentDirection = down;
static const int down = 0, left = 1, up = 2,
    right = 3;
```

As you can see, the variable naming is more generic now in this base class.

8. Next, we will migrate the three functions (changeDirection, update, and onCollision) from the George class to the Character class.

First, we will add the changeDirection function:

```
void changeDirection() {
    Random random = new Random();
    int newDirection = random.nextInt(4);

    switch (newDirection) {
        case down:
            animation = downAnimation;
            break;
        case left:
            animation = leftAnimation;
```

```
        break;
      case up:
        animation = upAnimation;
        break;
      case right:
        animation = rightAnimation;
        break;
    }

    currentDirection = newDirection;
  }
```

Now that we have added `changeDirection`, let's add the `update` function:

```
  @override
  void update(double deltaTime) {
    super.update(deltaTime);

    elapsedTime += deltaTime;
    if (elapsedTime > 3.0) {
      changeDirection();
      elapsedTime = 0.0;
    }
    switch (currentDirection) {
      case down:
        position.y += speed * deltaTime;
        break;
      case left:
        position.x -= speed * deltaTime;
        break;
      case up:
        position.y -= speed * deltaTime;
        break;
      case right:
        position.x += speed * deltaTime;
        break;
    }
  }
```

Next, let's add the onCollision function:

```
@override
void onCollision(Set<Vector2> points,
  Collidable other) {
  if (other is ScreenCollidable) {
    switch (currentDirection) {
      case down:
        currentDirection = up;
        animation = upAnimation;
        break;
      case left:
        currentDirection = right;
        animation = rightAnimation;
        break;
      case up:
        currentDirection = down;
        animation = downAnimation;
        break;
      case right:
        currentDirection = left;
        animation = leftAnimation;
        break;
    }
    elapsedTime = 0.0;
  }
}
```

As you can see from these three functions, they have the same functionality that we have in the George class, but we have named the variables to be more generic now, which is better for a base class.

Because we created an extension function for the George class for creating animations by columns, we will bring that over to the character.dart file too. The function will be available to use in all our sprites so that we can either create them by column or row.

After the class definition for the `Character` base class and at the bottom of the
`character.dart` file, add the extension code for `createAnimationByColumn`:

```
extension CreateAnimationByColumn on SpriteSheet {

    SpriteAnimation createAnimationByColumn({
      required int column,
      required double stepTime,
      bool loop = true,
      int from = 0,
      int? to,
    }) {
    to ??= columns;

    final spriteList =
      List<int>.generate(to - from, (i) => from + i)
      .map((e) => getSprite(e, column))
      .toList();

    return SpriteAnimation.spriteList(
      spriteList,
      stepTime: stepTime,
      loop: loop,
    );
  }
}
```

Now we have our `Character` base component set up, this makes the `George` class
a lot simpler.

9. In the `George` class, delete all the code and replace it with the following:

```
import 'package:flame/components.dart';
import 'package:flame/flame.dart';
import 'package:flame/geometry.dart';
import 'package:flame/sprite.dart';
import 'package:goldrush/components/character.dart';
class George extends Character {
  George({required Vector2 position,
```

```
    required Vector2 size, required double speed}) :
      super(position: position, size: size,
        speed: speed);

  @override
  Future<void> onLoad() async {
    super.onLoad();
    var spriteImages =
      await Flame.images.load('george.png');
    final spriteSheet = SpriteSheet(image:
      spriteImages, srcSize: Vector2(width, height));

    downAnimation =
      spriteSheet.createAnimationByColumn(column: 0,
        stepTime: 0.2);
    leftAnimation =
      spriteSheet.createAnimationByColumn(column: 1,
        stepTime: 0.2);
    upAnimation =
      spriteSheet.createAnimationByColumn(column: 2,
        stepTime: 0.2);
    rightAnimation =
      spriteSheet.createAnimationByColumn(column: 3,
        stepTime: 0.2);

    changeDirection();

    addHitbox(HitboxRectangle());
  }
}
```

As you can see, we only need to load the sprite sheet and set up the animations and we're good to go. It's a lot less code and much cleaner now it inherits the direction, movement, and collision code from the base class.

10. Now, let's set up a class for the zombie. In the `components` folder, create a new file called `zombie.dart` and add the following code:

```dart
import 'package:flame/components.dart';
import 'package:flame/flame.dart';
import 'package:flame/geometry.dart';
import 'package:flame/sprite.dart';
import 'package:goldrush/components/character.dart';

class Zombie extends Character {
  Zombie({required Vector2 position, required Vector2
    size, required double speed}) : super(position:
      position, size: size, speed: speed);

  @override
  Future<void> onLoad() async {
    super.onLoad();
    var spriteImages = await
      Flame.images.load('zombie_n_skeleton.png');
    final spriteSheet = SpriteSheet(image:
      spriteImages, srcSize: size);

    downAnimation = spriteSheet.createAnimation(
      row: 0, stepTime: 0.2, from: 0, to: 2);
    leftAnimation = spriteSheet.createAnimation(
      row: 1, stepTime: 0.2, from: 0, to: 2);
    upAnimation = spriteSheet.createAnimation(
      row: 3, stepTime: 0.2, from: 0, to: 2);
    rightAnimation = spriteSheet.createAnimation(
      row: 2, stepTime: 0.2, from: 0, to: 2);

    changeDirection();

    addHitbox(HitboxRectangle());
  }
}
```

Once again, the amount of code is small, just setting up the animation in the `onLoad` function. As it extends the `Character` class, we get all the same code we have for George too.

The main difference here is we use the built-in sprite sheet's `createAnimation` function instead of our extension function, as this sprite sheet is in rows and not columns. For the zombies, the animation frames are from columns 0 to 2, so we add those parameters in the `createAnimation` call too.

11. Now, let's set up the skeleton enemy. In the `components` folder, create a new file called `skeleton.dart` and add the following code:

```dart
import 'package:flame/components.dart';
import 'package:flame/flame.dart';
import 'package:flame/geometry.dart';
import 'package:flame/sprite.dart';
import 'package:goldrush/components/character.dart';

class Skeleton extends Character {
  Skeleton({required Vector2 position, required
    Vector2 size, required double speed}) : super(
      position: position, size: size, speed: speed);

  @override
  Future<void> onLoad() async {
    super.onLoad();
    var spriteImages = await
      Flame.images.load('zombie_n_skeleton.png');
    final spriteSheet = SpriteSheet(
      image: spriteImages, srcSize: size);

    downAnimation = spriteSheet.createAnimation(
      row: 0, stepTime: 0.2, from: 3, to: 5);
    leftAnimation = spriteSheet.createAnimation(
      row: 1, stepTime: 0.2, from: 3, to: 5);
    upAnimation = spriteSheet.createAnimation(
      row: 3, stepTime: 0.2, from: 3, to: 5);
    rightAnimation = spriteSheet.createAnimation(
```

```
        row: 2, stepTime: 0.2, from: 3, to: 5);

    changeDirection();

    addHitbox(HitboxRectangle());
  }
}
```

As with the zombie code, it's compact and inherits most functionality from the `Character` component. Because of the way the sprite sheet image is set up, we set the `from` and `to` fields to 3 to 5, respectively, to grab the correct animation frames for the skeleton.

Now we have the zombies and skeletons set up, let's add some extra collision code to the `George` class so that every time the `George` sprite collides with either a zombie or skeleton, it will delete the enemy from the screen as if the enemy had been killed.

12. At the bottom of the `George` class, add the following `onCollision` function:

```
@override
void onCollision(Set<Vector2> points,
  Collidable other) {
  super.onCollision(points, other);

  if (other is Zombie || other is Skeleton) {
    other.removeFromParent();
  }
}
```

13. Next, add the imports at the top of the `George` file for the `Zombie` and `Skeleton` classes:

```
import 'package:goldrush/components/skeleton.dart';
import 'package:goldrush/components/zombie.dart';
```

14. Finally, let's add the same imports that we just added to the `George` file to the `main.dart` file. Then, in the `onLoad` function, let's add the following code to add some zombies and skeletons and update George to pass the position, size, and speed:

```
add(George(position: Vector2(200, 400),
  size: Vector2(48.0, 48.0), speed: 40.0));
```

```
add (Zombie(position: Vector2(100, 200), size:
   Vector2(32.0, 64.0), speed: 20.0));
add (Zombie(position: Vector2(300, 200), size:
   Vector2(32.0, 64.0), speed: 20.0));
add (Skeleton(position: Vector2(100, 600), size:
   Vector2(32.0, 64.0), speed: 60.0));
add (Skeleton(position: Vector2(300, 600), size:
   Vector2(32.0, 64.0), speed: 60.0));
```

If you run the code now, you will see a few zombies and skeletons and George wandering around, randomly changing direction every few seconds and when they hit the edges. If George collides with an enemy, the enemy will be removed from the screen.

Here is a picture of how the game looks so far:

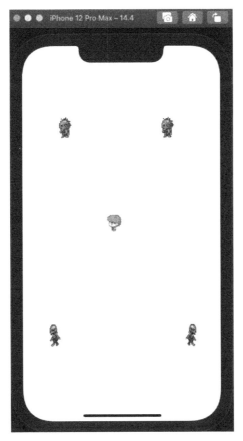

Figure 4.4 – George and the enemy sprites

In this section, we added enemy sprites to the game and collision code to detect when George collides with the enemies. We extracted the common code for movement and animation changes to a base class called `Character` and then built the sprite classes using this.

Summary

In this chapter, we showed you how to load graphics from a sprite sheet and extract and play the animations. Then, we showed you how to move the sprites around and change the animation to match the direction of travel. Finally, we showed you how to animate multiple sprites independently and detect when they collide with each other or the screen edges.

In the next chapter, we will add more interactivity by learning how to control your player character with virtual joysticks and buttons. We will also look at other methods of input control, including detecting touch events on the screen and using them to control the player character.

Questions

1. What is a sprite?

2. What functions should we use for the code which initializes the animations?

3. What are the benefits of using `SpriteAnimationComponent`?

4. What parameters should you set in the `createAnimation` function to specify a range within a sprite sheet?

5. What is the benefit of creating a base class for all our sprites?

5
Moving the Graphics with Input

In this chapter, we will take control of our own character and move them around the screen with virtual joysticks and touch events, so the player can choose where they want to move their character.

We will start by looking at how to draw onscreen controls that behave like a thumbstick on a PlayStation controller, with action buttons for things such as attacking and jumping. Next, we will connect the virtual controls with our George sprite and get him moving around the screen. And finally, we will discuss an alternative or addition to virtual controls, by controlling George with touch events, such as tapping on the screen and moving George to a tapped location.

So, we will cover the following topics:

- Drawing onscreen controls
- Moving our character with onscreen controls
- Moving our character with touch

Technical requirements

To examine the source from this chapter, you can download it from `https://github.com/PacktPublishing/Building-Games-with-Flutter/tree/main/chapter05`.

You can find additional information on Flame input in the online documentation at `https://docs.flame-engine.org/1.0.0/gesture-input.html` and `https://docs.flame-engine.org/1.0.0/other-inputs.html`.

In the next section, we will start by adding the onscreen controls and drawing them on the screen.

Drawing onscreen controls

In this section, we will add a joystick and a button to the screen that will allow us to control the character and some text for showing the player their score. These three components will form part of our **Heads-Up Display** (**HUD**), which is part of the user interface, showing game information that is drawn over the other graphics in the game and remains in a fixed position. The type of information could be the player's health, the number of lives remaining, or, in our case, the game score.

We will encapsulate our HUD into a single component, which makes showing or hiding it easier. The HUD component will contain `JoyStickComponent` for controlling the direction that George moves; the joystick will work by dragging an onscreen circle within a larger circle in the direction you want to move. The HUD will also include `HudButtonComponent`, an onscreen button that the player can press to double George's walking speed, making him run.

We will connect the HUD components in the next section, but for now, let's draw them on the screen:

1. First, create a folder inside the components folder called `hud` to hold our components.

2. Inside the hud folder, create four files called `hud.dart`, `joystick.dart`, `run_button.dart`, and `score_text.dart`.

3. In the `run_button.dart` file, add the following imports and class definition:

```
import 'package:flame/components.dart';
import 'package:flame/input.dart';
import 'package:flutter/material.dart';
```

```
class RunButton extends HudButtonComponent {
}
```

4. Next, we will add the constructor inside the class definition; this will include the values we need to pass to the HudButtonComponent base class via a call with super:

```
RunButton({
  required button,
  buttonDown,
  EdgeInsets? margin,
  Vector2? position,
  Vector2? size,
  Anchor anchor = Anchor.center,
  onPressed,
}) : super(
  button: button,
  buttonDown: buttonDown,
  margin: margin,
  position: position,
  size: size ?? button.size,
  anchor: anchor,
  onPressed: onPressed
);
```

5. Below this constructor, let's add a Boolean variable to keep track of whether this button is pressed or not, the default being false:

```
bool buttonPressed = false;
```

6. HudButtonComponent has a mixin called Tappable that allows us to detect when this button is pressed on the screen and override callbacks for onTapUp, onTapDown, and onTapCancel, which we will use to update the buttonPressed Boolean. Let's add these functions after the buttonPressed definition:

```
@override
bool onTapDown(TapDownInfo info) {
  super.onTapDown(info);
```

```
    buttonPressed = true;

    return true;
  }

  @override
  bool onTapUp(TapUpInfo info) {
    super.onTapUp(info);

    buttonPressed = false;

    return false;
  }

  @override
  bool onTapCancel() {
    super.onTapCancel();

    buttonPressed = false;

    return true;
  }
```

We will use RunButton in the HUD component in the hud.dart file, but for now, let's move on to defining TextComponent for our score.

7. Open the score_text.dart file and add the following imports and class definition:

```
import 'package:flame/components.dart';
import 'package:flame/input.dart';
import 'package:flame/palette.dart';
import 'package:flutter/cupertino.dart';

class ScoreText extends HudMarginComponent {
}
```

Note here that the ScoreText class extends HudMarginComponent and not TextComponent. This is because we want to place TextComponent with margins around it. We will create TextComponent inside this class, add it as a child component of HudMarginComponent, and pass the margins into the class via the constructor, which we will add next.

8. Add the following constructor inside the class to pass the margins to the class:

```
ScoreText({EdgeInsets? margin}) : super (margin: margin);
```

9. Below the constructor, add the following variables for score and the TextComponent child:

```
int score = 0;
String scoreText = "Score: ";

late TextPaint _regularPaint;
late TextComponent scoreTextComponent;
```

10. Below these variables, let's add the onLoad function, which is called when the component is first used, to set up TextComponent:

```
@override
Future<void> onLoad() async {
  super.onLoad();

  TextStyle textStyle = TextStyle(color:
    BasicPalette.blue.color, fontSize: 30.0);
  regularPaint = TextPaint(style: textStyle);
  scoreTextComponent = TextComponent(text: scoreText +
    score.toString(), textRenderer: _regularPaint);
  add(scoreTextComponent);
}
```

Here, we are setting the text color to blue and adding scoreTextComponent as a child to ScoreText.

11. Finally, for TextComponent, we want to expose a function for updating the score that will get updated every time George collides with one of the enemy sprites. So, let's add the setScore function below the onLoad function:

```
setScore(int score) {
  this.score += score;
  scoreTextComponent.text =
    scoreText + this.score.toString();
}
```

12. Next, we will add a simple JoystickComponent for controlling George's movement. To do that, open the joystick.dart file and add the following code:

```
import 'package:flame/components.dart';
import 'package:flutter/material.dart';

class Joystick extends JoystickComponent {
  Joystick({required PositionComponent knob,
    PositionComponent? background, EdgeInsets?
      margin}) : super (knob: knob, background:
        background, margin: margin);
}
```

We will keep this simple for now, but it's worth keeping JoystickComponent in its own file in case you want to style it more later, by using custom images for the joystick instead of colors.

13. Now that we have our joystick, run button, and score text components, let's create a HUD component that will handle the initialization of these components. First, open the hud.dart file and add the following imports and class definition:

```
import 'package:flame/components.dart';
import
  'package:goldrush/components/hud/run_button.dart';
import
  'package:goldrush/components/hud/score_text.dart';
import
  'package:goldrush/components/hud/joystick.dart';
import 'package:flame/palette.dart';
```

```
import 'package:flutter/material.dart';

class HudComponent extends PositionComponent {
}
```

Here, we extend from `PositionComponent`, giving us control over how we arrange our child components with margins. `PositionComponent` is a base class that allows the positioning of components within it.

14. At the top of the `HudComponent` class, let's add a constructor that sets `priority` to `20`:

```
HudComponent() : super(priority: 20);
```

`priority` is used to indicate the order components are drawn, with the default being `0`. So, setting this higher than `0` will ensure that the HUD is drawn on top of everything else.

Later, when we start using a map that is larger than the physical screen, the character and enemies will move around the map, but we want the score to stay at the top left of the screen while the map scrolls around.

15. Below this, we now define the variables to hold our child components:

```
late Joystick joystick;
late RunButton runButton;
late ScoreText scoreText;
```

16. Now, set these child components up on the `onLoad` function:

```
@override
Future<void> onLoad() async {
  super.onLoad();
  final joystickKnobPaint =
    BasicPalette.blue.withAlpha(200).paint();
  final joystickBackgroundPaint =
    BasicPalette.blue.withAlpha(100).paint();
  final buttonRunPaint =
    BasicPalette.red.withAlpha(200).paint();
```

```
final buttonDownRunPaint =
  BasicPalette.red.withAlpha(100).paint();

joystick = Joystick(
knob: CircleComponent(radius: 20.0, paint:
  joystickKnobPaint),
background: CircleComponent(radius: 40.0, paint:
  joystickBackgroundPaint),
  margin: const EdgeInsets.only(left: 40, bottom:
    40),
);

runButton = RunButton(
button: CircleComponent(radius: 25.0, paint:
  buttonRunPaint),
buttonDown: CircleComponent(radius: 25.0, paint:
  buttonDownRunPaint),
margin: const EdgeInsets.only(right: 20, bottom:
  50),
  onPressed: () => {}
);

scoreText = ScoreText(margin: const
  EdgeInsets.only(left: 40, top: 60));

add(joystick);
add(runButton);
add(scoreText);

positionType = PositionType.viewport;
}
```

Here, we set up some `Paint` objects for the colors of the components.

Next, we set up the joystick, using circles for the knob and background, and set the margin at the bottom left of the screen where the joystick will be located.

Then, we set up the run button in a similar way, with its margin at the bottom right to draw it opposite the joystick.

We then set the score text up with the margin at the top left of the screen.

After that, we add the HUD components and set `positionType` to `PositionType.viewport`.

`PositionType` ensures that this component is drawn on top of everything, even if the game camera moves around.

Please note that for the run button, it takes a function callback for when the button is pressed, but because we are managing the tap handling ourselves in the run button class, we can just ignore this and pass { } instead.

17. Let's add our `HudComponent` to the game so we can see our new components. Open the `main.dart` file and add the following import to the top of the file:

    ```
    import 'package:goldrush/components/hud/hud.dart';
    ```

18. At the top of the `onLoad` function, let's add our `HudComponent`:

    ```
    add(HudComponent());
    ```

19. As the `HudComponent` class contains components that are draggable (`Joystick`) and tappable (`RunButton`), we must pass the mixins for `HasDraggables` and `HasTappables` to the class definition for `MyGame`:

    ```
    class MyGame extends FlameGame with HasCollidables,
    HasDraggables, HasTappables {
    ```

If you run the game now, you will see the new components displayed with the existing game sprites:

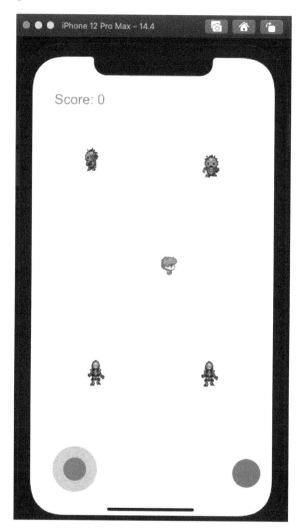

Figure 5.1 – The game with the HUD controls

In this section, we learned how to add a joystick, a button, and a score to our game and positioned them on the screen.

In the next section, we will connect the joystick to George's movement and make him run faster when the run button is pressed. We will also update the score by 10 when George collides with an enemy.

Moving our character with onscreen controls

In this section, we will start by connecting George's movement to the joystick.

Currently, the George class inherits his movement from the base class, Character, which it shares with the Skeleton and Zombie classes. As George will have different movement code from the enemy sprites, let's refactor the code to allow the enemy sprites' movement code. We will move the existing movement code into an EnemyCharacter class, which will become the new base class for the enemy sprites and remove this code from the Character class.

Let's get started:

1. In the components folder, create a file called character_enemy.dart.

2. Open the file and add the code at https://github.com/PacktPublishing/Building-Games-with-Flutter/blob/main/chapter05/lib/components/character_enemy.dart.

   In this code, the EnemyCharacter class extends our Character class, and we have copied the onCollision, update, and changeDirection functions straight from the Character class.

3. In the changeDirection function in the EnemyCharacter class, you will need to update the switch case block to prepend the directions with the Character base class. Once done, the block will look like this:

```
switch (newDirection) {
  case Character.down:
    animation = downAnimation;
    break;
  case Character.left:
    animation = leftAnimation;
    break;
  case Character.up:
    animation = upAnimation;
    break;
  case Character.right:
    animation = rightAnimation;
    break;
}
```

4. Open the `zombie.dart` and `skeleton.dart` files, and inside them both, instead of extending from `Character`, change the class definition to extend from `EnemyCharacter`.

5. Remove the previous import for `character.dart` and replace this with the following:

    ```
    import 'character_enemy.dart';
    ```

6. Open the `character.dart` class and remove the functions for `onCollision`, `update`, and `changeDirection` that we now have in the `EnemyCharacter` class. You can also remove the import for the `math` package now too.

7. Open the file for `george.dart` and remove the line for `changeDirection` in the `onLoad` function.

8. If you run the game now, you will see George is invisible because we have not updated him and set his animation yet. Let's fix that by adding the following code in the `onLoad` function in the `george.dart` file:

    ```
    animation = downAnimation;
    playing = false;
    ```

9. Next, we will set up some variables for `walkingSpeed` and `runningSpeed` that will be toggled when the run button is pressed. At the top of the `George` class, below the constructor, add the following variables:

    ```
    late double walkingSpeed, runningSpeed;
    ```

10. Then, at the top of the `onLoad` function, let's set `walkingSpeed` to equal the default speed that the sprite will move at and `runningSpeed` to be twice as fast:

    ```
    walkingSpeed = speed;
    runningSpeed = speed * 2;
    ```

11. Because we want to read the status on the joystick and the run button, we need to get a reference to `HudComponent`. So, let's pass the HUD via the constructor and store the HUD in a variable:

    ```
    final HudComponent hud;
    ```

12. Then, update the constructor to pass the HUD so that we can access the values from the HUD in this class:

```
George({required this.hud, required Vector2 position,
required Vector2 size, required double speed}) :
super(position: position, size: size, speed: speed);
```

13. Next, we need to add the import for `HudComponent`:

```
import 'package:goldrush/components/hud/hud.dart';
```

14. Now, we will add the `update` function below the `onCollision` function and connect the run button to the `speed` variable:

```
@override
void update(double dt) {
  super.update(dt);

  speed = hud.runButton.buttonPressed ?
    runningSpeed : walkingSpeed;
}
```

If the run button is pressed, the speed will be `runningSpeed`; otherwise, it will be `walkingSpeed`.

15. After the line that sets the speed for walking and running, let's add the code that links the joystick to the character's movements and set the character's direction and animation based on the direction of the joystick:

```
if (!hud.joystick.delta.isZero()) {
  position.add(hud.joystick.relativeDelta * speed
    * dt);
  playing = true;

  switch (hud.joystick.direction) {
    case JoystickDirection.up:
    case JoystickDirection.upRight:
    case JoystickDirection.upLeft:
      animation = upAnimation;
      currentDirection = Character.up;
    break;
```

```
        case JoystickDirection.down:
        case JoystickDirection.downRight:
        case JoystickDirection.downLeft:
          animation = downAnimation;
          currentDirection = Character.down;
        break;

        case JoystickDirection.left:
          animation = leftAnimation;
          currentDirection = Character.left;
        break;
        case JoystickDirection.right:
          animation = rightAnimation;
          currentDirection = Character.right;
        break;
        case JoystickDirection.idle:
          animation = null;
        break;
      }
    } else {
    if (playing) {
      stopAnimations();
    }
  }
}
```

Here, if the joystick reading is 0, the character doesn't move, but if it is above 0, the character is moving. If the joystick is moving, we update our position based on the value from the joystick, the current speed, and deltaTime. Then, based on the joystick direction, we set the correct direction and animation. If there is no joystick movement, we check whether the animation is playing; if it is, we will call stopAnimations, which we will define next.

16. At the bottom of the class, we will create a new function called stopAnimations with the following code:

```
void stopAnimations() {
  animation?.currentIndex = 0;
  playing = false;
}
```

The stopAnimations function stops the animation from playing by setting the variable to false and sets the current animation index to 0; this draws the first frame of the animation as a static image. This gives the impression that we animate the character while the joystick is being used and the character George stands still when we stop using the joystick.

17. Let's increase the score by 10 every time an enemy is killed. In the onCollision function, update the function like so to increase the score:

```
if (other is Zombie || other is Skeleton) {
  other.removeFromParent();
  hud.scoreText.setScore(10);
}
```

18. Finally, open the main.dart file and update the onLoad function so that we create HudComponent as its own variable. This is used to store the HUD value that is passed to the George class as a parameter:

```
@override
Future<void> onLoad() async {
  var hud = HudComponent();
  add(Background());
  add (George(hud: hud, position: Vector2(200, 400),
    size: Vector2(48.0, 48.0), speed: 40.0));
  add (Zombie(position: Vector2(100, 200),
    size: Vector2(32.0, 64.0), speed: 20.0));
  add (Zombie(position: Vector2(300, 200),
    size: Vector2(32.0, 64.0), speed: 20.0));
  add (Skeleton(position: Vector2(100, 600),
    size: Vector2(32.0, 64.0), speed: 60.0));
  add (Skeleton(position: Vector2(300, 600),
    size: Vector2(32.0, 64.0), speed: 60.0));
  add(ScreenCollidable());
  add(hud);
}
```

If you run the app now, you will be able to control George with the joystick and chase down and kill the enemies much quicker when you collide with them. If you press and hold the run button while you are controlling the joystick, you will see George move at his running speed.

In this section, we added a HUD containing a joystick, run button, and score text, which we connected to the game to control George's movement and update the score when George kills an enemy.

In the next section, we will show you an alternative way to control George instead of using the joystick control, by detecting touch events on the screen and then moving George to that location.

Moving our character with touch

Now that we have George moving with the joystick, let's look at an alternative method for moving our character via screen touch events, which is very popular in games. With mobile devices having very sensitive high-resolution screens nowadays, we can use touch events or gestures to move our character from its current location to the location on the screen that was tapped. Using trigonometry, we can calculate the angle between the origin and target locations and use the angle to move George in the correct direction, with the correct animation that matches the direction.

We are already detecting a tap event for the run button via the `HasTappables` mixin. So, to detect touches on the screen, we need to add the `Tappable` mixin to the `Background` class and override `onTapUp` to get an *x* and *y* location that we can use to calculate the movement.

Because we need to know this coordinate inside of the `George` class, we will need to pass in a reference to the `George` class into the `Background` class so that we can pass the tap event when the player touches the screen.

To get started, let's modify the `Background` class:

1. Open the `background.dart` file. Add the following constructor and variable for holding the reference to the `George` class at the top of the class. We will use this for passing events back to the `George` class when the player touches the screen, and we will call a function on the `George` class called `moveToLocation` and pass the tap event:

    ```
    Background(this.george);
    final George george;
    ```

2. Resolve the reference to the `George` class with this import:

    ```
    import 'george.dart';
    ```

3. Change the `Background` class definition by adding the `Tappable` mixin:

    ```
    class Background extends PositionComponent with Tappable
    {
    ```

4. Add the following code to the bottom of the class to override the onTapUp function and pass the TapUpInfo event to the George class:

```
@override
bool onTapUp(TapUpInfo info) {
  george.moveToLocation(info);
  return true;
}
```

At the moment, the moveToLocation function doesn't exist in the George class, but we will add that later when we update the George class. Because we are going to use the touch event, we return true from this function to indicate that the touch event was handled.

5. Add the following import to resolve the TapUpInfo reference:

```
import 'package:flame/input.dart';
```

6. In the main.dart file's onLoad function, let's make the George class into a variable, and then we can pass that into the Background class constructor. To do this, change the first few lines on the onLoad function like this:

```
@override
Future<void> onLoad() async {
  var hud = HudComponent();
  var george = George(hud: hud, position:
    Vector2(200, 400), size: Vector2(48.0, 48.0),
      speed: 40.0);
  add(Background(george));
  add (george);
```

Note that only the top part of the onLoad function is presented here to show the changed lines, but the rest of the lines that add the enemies, HUD, and ScreenCollidable are left the same.

Before we make the final changes to the George class, let's create a math utility class for storing a function to get the angle between George's location and the location on the screen where the player touches.

7. In the lib folder, create a new folder called utils, and in that folder, create a new file called math_utils.dart.

8. Open the new `math_utils.dart` file and add the following code for the `getAngle` function:

```dart
import 'dart:math';
import 'package:flame/components.dart';

double getAngle(Vector2 origin, Vector2 target) {
  double dx = target.x - origin.x;
  double dy = -(target.y - origin.y);
  double angleInRadians = atan2(dy, dx);

  if (angleInRadians < 0) {
    angleInRadians = angleInRadians.abs();
  }
  else {
    angleInRadians = 2 * pi - angleInRadians;
  }
  return angleInRadians * radians2Degrees;
}
```

We are not going to go into much detail about how the `getAngle` function works, but it uses basic trigonometry covered in most high school math classes. The `getAngle` function will return an angle between 0 and 360, with 0 degrees facing right, 90 degrees facing down, 180 degrees facing left, and 270 degrees facing up.

9. Open the `george.dart` file and add the following imports for the math utilities class:

```dart
import 'package:goldrush/utils/math_utils.dart';
```

10. In the `George` class, after the constructor, let's add a couple of variables for the `targetLocation` vector and a variable to track whether we are moving via touch:

```dart
late Vector2 targetLocation;
bool movingToTouchedLocation = false;
```

11. Now, let's add the `moveToLocation` function we referenced earlier in the `Background` component, set `targetLocation` to the touch event that was passed, and set `movingToTouchedLocation` to `true`:

```dart
void moveToLocation(TapUpInfo info) {
  targetLocation = info.eventPosition.game;
```

```
            movingToTouchedLocation = true;
        }
```

Sprites have an anchor point that defaults to the top left of the sprite in Flame, so if we touch on the screen the sprite would be moved and the top-left corner of the sprite would align with the touched point on the screen. It feels more natural to center the sprite around the center of the sprite rather than the top left, so let's update the anchor point to be in the center.

12. At the bottom of the `onLoad` function and before adding the hitbox, add the following code to set the anchor in the center of the sprite.

```
anchor = Anchor.center;


addHitbox(HitboxRectangle());
```

13. Finally, we are going to add code to our `update` function that will move George to the touched location. In the `update` function, look for the `else` block containing the following code:

```
if (playing) {
    stopAnimations();
}
```

Replace it with this code block:

```
if (movingToTouchedLocation) {
    } else {
        if (playing) {
            stopAnimations();
        }
    }
```

14. Inside the `if` code block, add the following code to set the new anchor position:

```
position += (targetLocation - position).normalized() *
(speed * dt);
```

This code updates George's position based on the difference between `targetLocation` and the current `position`, while taking account of the current `speed` and the time since the last update was called, to ensure the movement is smooth.

15. When we arrive at the touched location, we want to stop any animations from playing and set `movedToTouchedLocation` to `false`. Because we are moving the character based on fractions that could have rounding issues, we allow for a small threshold value in deciding whether George is near enough to the touched location, and if he is, we stop the animations. So, let's continue inside this code block and add the check for the threshold:

```
double threshold = 1.0;
var difference = targetLocation - position;
if (difference.x.abs() < threshold &&
  difference.y.abs() < threshold) {
  stopAnimations();
  movingToTouchedLocation = false;
  return;
}
```

16. Finally, we will use the `getAngle` function we created earlier and use the angle to decide what direction George is moving in and which is the closest animation to this. For instance, we only have four animations – up, down, left, and right – so we will approximate the direction by splitting the directions into four 90-degree quadrants, illustrated by the following diagram:

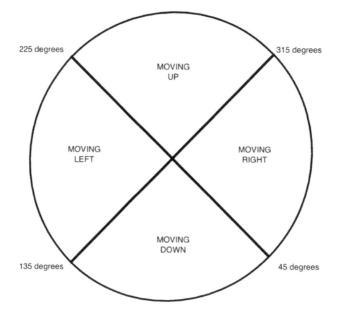

Figure 5.2 – The quadrant mapping to move direction

Based on our diagram, if we are moving between 45 degrees and 135 degrees, we are approximately moving down, so we can set the direction to down and use downAnimation to animate the sprite correctly. Remember that 0 degrees points east, and we need 2 checks for moving right, between 315 to 360 degrees and 0 to 45 degrees. So, let's add code for this logic, continuing in the same code block:

```
playing = true;
var angle = getAngle(position, targetLocation);
if ((angle > 315 && angle < 360) || (angle > 0
  && angle < 45) ) { // Moving right
  animation = rightAnimation;
  currentDirection = Character.right;
}
// Moving down
else if (angle > 45 && angle < 135) {
  animation = downAnimation;
  currentDirection = Character.down;
}
// Moving left
else if (angle > 135 && angle < 225) {
  animation = leftAnimation;
  currentDirection = Character.left;
}
// Moving up
else if (angle > 225 && angle < 315) {
  animation = upAnimation;
  currentDirection = Character.up;
}
```

Now, if you run the code, you can control George by touching anywhere on the screen, and he will move there. You can also use the joystick if you want to. Whichever movement method you prefer, the run button will still make George run faster while pressed. Also, note that if you use touch to move the character and then switch to joystick control, it will interrupt the movement caused by the touch, allowing you to manually control George's movement.

Summary

We covered a lot in this chapter, and the game is really starting to take shape. We learned how to create onscreen controls for our game with a joystick and a run button, as well as how to add text on the screen for our score. We then learned an alternative method for controlling George by allowing you to touch the screen to move him to the touched location.

The game is a bit quiet at the moment, though. In most games, music soundtracks and sound effects are used to create atmosphere and bring them to life. In the next chapter, we will add some music and sounds to the game to enhance it further.

Questions

1. What is a HUD and what is it used for in our game?

2. Which mixin do we use to convert a component to detect when it is touched?

3. What component do we use to draw text on the screen?

4. Why do you think `JoystickComponent` needs the `HasDraggables` mixin?

6
Playing Sound Effects and Music

In this chapter, we will bring our game to life by adding sound effects and music that will enhance the game. Audio is a very important part of any game; it can alert you to key events happening in a game or create atmosphere. Imagine walking through a forest in a game and hearing a nearby river or the birds singing in the trees. It makes the whole game more immersive if the sound matches what you would expect to hear if you were in that forest.

It is important though that if the player puts the game in the background to, for example, check their email, that we stop the music or sound from playing, and that the sound resumes when they return to the game, otherwise the ongoing sound could be annoying for the player. To handle this, we will cover how to listen for these life cycle events so that we ensure the audio is paused and resumed correctly.

Audio also takes up memory and we will discuss how Flame uses an audio cache to help load and keep these audio resources so we can play them whenever we need them in a game. Often, sound effects are played multiple times, so we need to be able to access these easily and play them repeatedly when needed.

So, in this chapter, we will cover the following topics:

- Playing background music

- Playing sound effects

- Controlling the volume

Technical requirements

To examine the source from this chapter, you can download it from `https://github.com/PacktPublishing/Building-Games-with-Flutter/tree/main/chapter06`.

You can find additional information on Flame audio in the online documentation at `https://docs.flame-engine.org/1.0.0/audio.html`.

To get started playing sounds and music in our game, we must download the asset files and add them to our `pubspec.yaml` file. We can find all the sound files we want to add at the excellent free website `https://freesound.org`.

The sound effects and music we want to add are the following:

- Background music playing throughout the game

- A sound effect for when an enemy dies

- A sound effect when George moves around

Here are some I found while browsing the site, but feel free to browse the site and find other sounds you may prefer:

- Background music – `https://github.com/PacktPublishing/Building-Games-with-Flutter/blob/main/chapter06/assets/audio/music/music.mp3`

- George movement – `https://github.com/PacktPublishing/Building-Games-with-Flutter/blob/main/chapter06/assets/audio/sounds/running.wav`

- Enemy dying – `https://github.com/PacktPublishing/Building-Games-with-Flutter/blob/main/chapter06/assets/audio/sounds/enemy_dies.wav`

In the following steps, we will download some sounds to use in our game:

1. Download the music and sound effects mentioned or find some of your own on the website.

2. Rename the music file to be called `music.mp3`, George's movement sound to be called `running.wav`, and the enemy dying sound to be called `enemy_dies.wav`.

3. Open the `assets` folder and create a new folder called `audio`.

4. In the `audio` folder, create a folder called `music` and a folder called `sounds`.

5. In the `music` folder, add the `music.mp3` file.

6. In the `sounds` folder, add the `enemy_dies.wav` and `running.wav` files.

7. Next, open the `pubspec.yaml` file and add the following assets below the existing assets that we have for the sprite images:

   ```
   - assets/audio/music/music.mp3
   - assets/audio/sounds/enemy_dies.wav
   - assets/audio/sounds/running.wav
   ```

8. Under the line where we added the Flame library, we will add a line for the Flame audio library, so your dependencies should now look like this:

   ```
   flame: 1.0.0
   flame_audio: ^1.0.0
   ```

9. Save this file, and `pub get` will update to validate the new assets and download the Flame audio library.

Now that we have the audio files set up as assets, let's add them to the game.

Playing background music

In this section, we will add the music playback, which will load at the start of the game and continue playing while we play the game. The Flame audio library has a static class called `Bgm` (background music) that adds music to the audio cache and will pause and resume the music when the app is backgrounded or brought back to the front. We get this functionality built into the `Bgm` class, so it requires very little code to get the music loaded and playing. As you will see in the next section regarding the playing of sound effects, we must do a bit more work to ensure sound effects pause and resume when backgrounded. Unfortunately, this is how it currently works in the Flame library at this time, but hopefully, this will be improved in future versions of the library.

To add the music playback to the code, do the following:

1. Open the `main.dart` file and import the `Flame` audio library:

    ```
    import 'package:flame_audio/flame_audio.dart';
    ```

2. At the top of the `onLoad` function, add the following code to initialize the library, load the music into the audio cache, and play the background music:

    ```
    FlameAudio.bgm.initialize();
    await FlameAudio.bgm.load('music/music.mp3');
    await FlameAudio.bgm.play('music/music.mp3');
    ```

3. In the `MyGame` class, below the `onLoad` function, add the following code, which stops playing the music and clears in the audio cache when the game closes:

    ```
    @override
    void onRemove() {
      FlameAudio.bgm.stop();
      FlameAudio.bgm.clearAll();

      super.onRemove();
    }
    ```

If you run the game now, you will hear our music playing. If you background the app on mobile, you will notice the music stops playing and will resume if you bring the game back to the foreground. If you close the game completely, by killing the app, you will notice the music also stops.

It is important to do these steps on the `onRemove` function so that we avoid memory leaks. In the next section, we will add sound effects to the game when we move George and when an enemy dies.

Playing sound effects

As mentioned in the previous section, when playing sound effects, we need to handle the pausing and resuming of the sound effects if they are still playing when the app is put in the background, for instance, to check something else on your phone, as this is not currently handled by the library.

We will initially update our `Character` class, which is our top-level base class for all our sprites, to add `onPaused` and `onResumed` callbacks, which all our sprites can use.

We will then listen for life cycle change events in our game and if these are called, we will iterate over all our sprites and pass on these events.

And finally, as the sound effects are related to George, we will update the George class to play sounds and pause and resume these sound effects when needed. Let's get started:

1. Open up the character.dart file. At the bottom of the Character class, add the following function definitions:

    ```
    void onPaused() {}
    void onResumed() {}
    ```

    Note that we will leave these functions empty as we will override these in the George class.

2. Open the main.dart file, and below the onRemove function that we recently added, add the following code to listen and handle life cycle events:

    ```
    @override
    void lifecycleStateChange(AppLifecycleState state) {
      switch(state) {
        case AppLifecycleState.paused:
          children.forEach((component) {
            if (component is Character) {
              component.onPaused();
            }
          });
          break;
        case AppLifecycleState.resumed:
          children.forEach((component) {
            if (component is Character) {
              component.onResumed();
            }
          });
          break;
        case AppLifecycleState.inactive:
        case AppLifecycleState.detached:
          break;
      }
    }
    ```

In the `lifecycleStateChange` function that we override, we are passing an `AppLifecycleState` event, which can be either a `paused`, `resumed`, `inactive`, or `detached` event. As we only care about the paused and resumed states, these are the only events we handle in this function.

Flame keeps track of all the children components we have added to the game in a variable called `children`, which is a set of data we can iterate over. Don't forget that `HudComponent` and `ScreenCollidable` are also components that will be in this dataset, so we must check when we iterate over the data that the class is of the `Character` type and ignore the other component types.

We can then safely pass on the pause and resume event via our `onPaused` and `onResumed` callbacks as we know these are available to any classes that use `Character` as a base class, such as our enemy sprites or George sprite.

3. Add the following import for the `Character` class:

    ```
    Import 'package:goldrush/components/character.dart';
    ```

4. Open the `george.dart` file and add the following imports:

    ```
    import 'package:flame_audio/flame_audio.dart';
    import 'package:audioplayers/audioplayers.dart';
    ```

5. The two sound effects we will play are when an enemy collides with George and when George walks or runs, controlled by the joystick or touch. If you have played the sounds that we downloaded, you will notice the enemy dying sound effect is short and the running sound effect is much longer. The challenge is that if George keeps moving longer than the sound effect lasts, we need to keep the sound playing by looping the sound.

    Also, as mentioned earlier, if the game is put in the background, we need to pause the sound and then resume it from the same point if the user returns to the game. Because of this, we need to store a reference to `AudioPlayer` returned when playing the long-looped audio returned from the running sound effect, meaning we have control over its playback.

    Let's create a couple of variables at the top of the `George` class that we have opened for tracking whether a user is moving and for accessing the audio player state:

    ```
    bool isMoving = false;
    late AudioPlayer audioPlayerRunning;
    ```

6. At the bottom of the `onLoad` function, let's load the sound effects into the audio cache:

    ```
    await FlameAudio.audioCache.loadAll(
      ['sounds/enemy_dies.wav', 'sounds/running.wav']);
    ```

    We use `await` on this line to wait until all the sound effect files are loaded into the cache.

7. At the bottom of the `onCollision` function after the code block that checks whether the other is a zombie or skeleton and sets the score, add the following code to play the enemy dies sound effect when we collide with an enemy:

    ```
    FlameAudio.play('sounds/enemy_dies.wav');
    ```

8. At the bottom of the `George` class, let's add the two functions for pausing and resuming `AudioPlayer` when the app is put in the background:

    ```
    @override
    void onPaused() {
      if (isMoving) {
        audioPlayerRunning.pause();
      }
    }

    @override
    void onResumed() async {
      if (isMoving) {
        audioPlayerRunning.resume();
      }
    }
    ```

9. In the `update` function, we have a few changes to make to play the long looping audio and to control it. In the code block at the top of the `update` function, where we are already checking whether the joystick has moved, let's add the following code where we set `playing = true;`, so it looks like this:

    ```
    playing = true;
    movingToTouchedLocation = false;

    if (!isMoving) {
      isMoving = true;
    ```

```
audioPlayerRunning = await
  FlameAudio.loopLongAudio('sounds/running.wav');
}
```

10. As we are waiting for the long-looped audio, we need to change the function signature to be asynchronous. Do this with the following change:

```
@override
void update(double dt) async {
```

11. In the `else` block, in the code block where we check whether `movingToTouchedLocation` is `true`, we will add the same code that we added for the joystick check, to start the audio playing and set the flag for `isMoving` to `true`:

```
} else {
  if (movingToTouchedLocation) {
    if (!isMoving) {
      isMoving = true;
      audioPlayerRunning = await
        FlameAudio.loopLongAudio('sounds/running.wav');
    }
```

Because we added the code in both locations, the running sound will start playing irrespective of whether the player controls George with either the joystick or by touch.

12. Further down this `update` function, where we called `stopAnimations` and set `movingToTouchedLocation` to `false` and `return`, let's stop the audio and set `isMoving` to `false`:

```
stopAnimations();

audioPlayerRunning.stop();
isMoving = false;

movingToTouchedLocation = false;
```

This code is within the code block where we check the threshold value and decide whether George is near enough to the touched location to stop him from moving.

13. At the bottom of the `update` function in the final `else` block, we will add the same `isMoving` check we added for the touched location check. This will stop the running sound effect when the user stops moving the joystick, so we have both the joystick and touch covered.

    The `else` block at the bottom of the function should now look like this:

    ```
    } else {
      if (playing) {
        stopAnimations();
      }
      if (isMoving) {
        isMoving = false;
        audioPlayerRunning.stop();
      }
    }
    ```

In this section, we added sound effects for George running and colliding with an enemy. We also added the correct handling for stopping the long-looped running sound when George stops moving or when the game is moved to the background.

If you run the game now, you will hear the background music playing but the sound effects may be difficult to hear at the same time because of the music playing too. This is because both the sound effects and music have the same default volume, making it difficult to hear them both clearly.

In the next section, we will adjust the volume of the sound effects and music to fix this issue and make it easier to hear the sound effects.

Controlling the volume

Fixing the volume of the music and sound effects is very easy and only requires a few small changes. Let's take a look:

1. Open the `main.dart` file. In the `onLoad` function, where we added the call to play the background music, change this line to pass the `volume` parameter:

    ```
    await FlameAudio.bgm.play('music/music.mp3',
      volume: 0.1);
    ```

Here we set the music volume to `0.1`, keeping it low so we can hear the sound effects better. The `volume` parameter can be any value between 0.0 and 1.0 (0.0 mutes the sound of the music or sound effect completely, whereas 1.0 plays the sound at full volume).

2. Open the `george.dart` file and let's update the calls to play each sound effect to use the `volume` parameter. In the `onCollision` function, update the enemy dying sound effect like this:

    ```
    FlameAudio.play('sounds/enemy_dies.wav', volume: 1.0);
    ```

3. In the `update` function, change the two calls to play the running sound effect, and add the `volume` parameter in both places:

    ```
    audioPlayerRunning = await FlameAudio.loopLongAudio(
      'sounds/running.wav', volume: 1.0);
    ```

If you run the game now, you will be able to hear the sound effects over the music.

Summary

In this chapter, we introduced music and sound effects to make the game better. We handled the playback and paused the sound when the app is in the background, and resumed it when the player returns to the game, by handling the life cycle events.

In the next chapter, we will go beyond the limits of the physical screen and learn how to make game levels that use maps that we can scroll around as we move around the map.

Questions

1. Which library do we use to add audio to our games?

2. Why is it beneficial to load the audio into the audio cache?

3. Why do we need to clear the audio buffer after the components are removed from the game?

4. Which life cycle change states do we need to handle when the game is backgrounded?

5. What class do we use to keep a reference to a longer sound effect?

6. How do we change the default volume for music or sound effects?

7
Designing Your Own Levels

So far, our game has used the physical limits of the device screen as the boundary for both George and our enemy sprites. In this chapter, we are going to show you how to make game levels that are bigger than the screen and how to scroll around the level using a camera to show part of the level.

We will show you how to add dynamic objects or sprites and how to deal with collisions on these larger levels. This is a very common technique and is used by most types of games, including platform games such as Sonic and 2D role-playing games such as Ultima or Zelda.

We will cover the following topics:

- Introduction to Tiled
- Loading a tile map
- Adding dynamic objects to the map
- Understanding map navigation
- Detecting tile collisions

Technical requirements

To examine the source from this chapter, you can download it from https://github.com/PacktPublishing/Building-Games-with-Flutter/tree/main/chapter07 by following these steps:

1. From https://github.com/PacktPublishing/Building-Games-with-Flutter/blob/main/chapter07/assets/images/tiles.png, download the tiles.png file and move it into the assets/images local project folder.

2. From https://github.com/PacktPublishing/Building-Games-with-Flutter/blob/main/chapter07/assets/tiles/tiles.tmx, download the tiles.tmx file.

    From https://github.com/PacktPublishing/Building-Games-with-Flutter/blob/main/chapter07/assets/tiles/tiles.tsx, download the tiles.tsx file.

    Then, move both files into the assets/tiles local project folder after creating this folder.

3. Open the pubspec.yaml file and add the following library dependency:

    ```
    flame_tiled: ^1.0.0
    ```

4. In the assets section of the same file, let's add the tile assets we just downloaded:

    ```
    - assets/tiles/tiles.tmx
    - assets/tiles/tiles.tsx
    - assets/images/tiles.png
    ```

5. Save the file and allow pub get to download this dependency and validate the assets:

    ```
    flutter pub get
    ```

Now that we have downloaded the required tile map files and dependencies, let's look into the software used to create tile maps.

Introduction to Tiled

Tiled is a free, open source, easy-to-use, and flexible level editor that can be downloaded from `https://www.mapeditor.org/`.

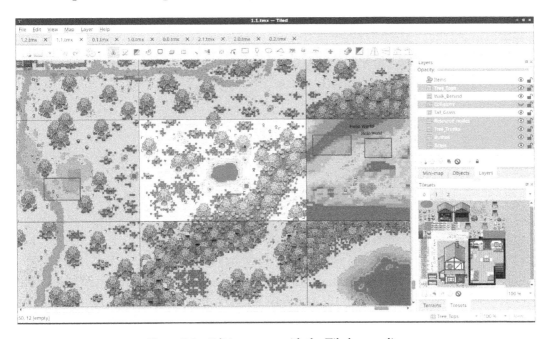

Figure 7.1 – Editing a map with the Tiled map editor

The levels we create with Tiled are known as tile maps. Tile maps are very common in 2D game development as they allow us to create large maps or levels out of fixed-size tiles.

A tile map is like a sprite sheet, which we have used before in *Chapter 4*, *Drawing and Animating Graphics*. The data is stored in one large image, and we extract what we need into smaller components.

This is a very performant and memory-efficient way of creating maps larger than the physical screen size. If you were to try and make this with a very large image, the image would need to be loaded into memory, which may cause the game to crash or run very slowly.

Let's look at an example of some graphics from a tile map and how they might be used. The following example is from the website `https://opengameart.org/content/tilecraft-tile-set-ground#`, which was made by user GrumpyDiamond.

As you can see in the following screenshot, it has different types of terrain that we can use to create a larger map:

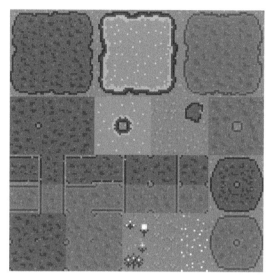

Figure 7.2 – An image containing various terrains

Sometimes, tile map images also contain buildings or trees that you can use on the maps too, but in this example, we see tiles for making water, grass, paths, and a few plants.

We can then load this image and break each image part into its smaller tiles, which can then be used to create a larger map, as in the following screenshot:

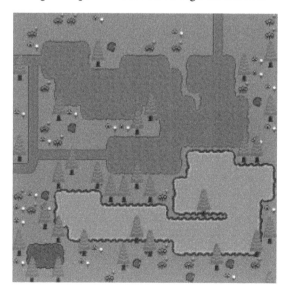

Figure 7.3 – Using the terrain images to make a larger map

Notice in *Figure 7.3* that a much larger water area was created by reusing the smaller tile images to build something much bigger.

The Tiled tool makes creating tile maps very easy, including tools such as image editing, which allow you to draw with tiles onto the map however you like. You can export maps from Tiled in a variety of formats, but XML and JSON are the most common.

Tiled is a tool that is easy to get started with but also has advanced features beyond the scope of this book, so we won't go into any more detail about it here. Instead, we will provide the premade tile maps for use in our game, so that you can use them directly, but I do recommend spending some time with Tiled once you want to create tile maps for your own games.

When you export a map from Tiled, it has a lot of information about the map and tile size, but the map data section is represented as a 2D array, which could look something like this:

```
[
  [1, 1, 1, 1, 1, 1, 1, 1],
  [1, 2, 2, 2, 2, 2, 2, 1],
  [1, 2, 3, 3, 3, 3, 2, 1],
  [1, 2, 2, 2, 2, 2, 2, 1],
  [1, 1, 1, 1, 1, 1, 1, 1]
]
```

The 2D array in the preceding code block is eight tiles wide and five tiles high. 1 in the array could represent the tile ID for some mountains, 2 might represent a path, and 3 might be water. So, in this example, the map has a path around a lake in the center of the map, with mountains around the outer edges.

Inside a game, we would load this data and iterate over the array and draw each visible tile based on its tile ID. We will draw the tiles starting at the top left, 0, 0, and then go through the tile data line by line, drawing each tile in turn.

Now that we have had an introduction to tile maps, we will add our own to the game in the next section.

Loading a tile map

In the *Technical requirements* section, we added our tile map files and the `flame_tiled` library, which is used for loading and displaying tile maps.

Each tile is 32 x 32 pixels, and the map is 50 tiles wide by 50 tiles high, so our total map size in pixels will be 1,600 x 1,600 pixels, which is 50 * 32 for width and height.

You can open the `tiles.tmx` file in Tiled if you want to see how the tile map looks there, but here is a screenshot of how our tile map looks when loaded and drawn:

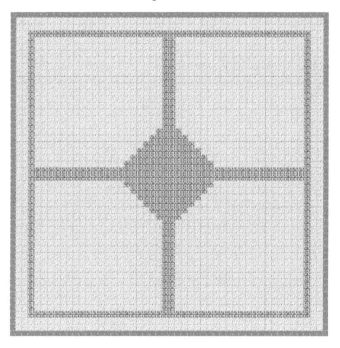

Figure 7.4 – The Gold Rush tile map

The map is basic with water around the edges and paths leading to the center of the map, with grass everywhere else on the map.

We will use this as our base, adding objects and enemies to the map and collision detection to the water areas to prevent George or the enemies from moving off the edges of the map.

Let's get started by loading the tile map and displaying it:

1. Open the `main.dart` file. In the `onLoad` function, we will add the following code to load the tile map into `TiledComponent` and make it a game component. Let's add this in the following code block, where we previously added the code for the `Background` component:

    ```
    add(Background(george));
    final tiledMap = await
      TiledComponent.load('tiles.tmx', Vector2.all(32));
    add(tiledMap);
    ```

2. Add the following import at the top of the file:

    ```
    import 'package:flame_tiled/flame_tiled.dart';
    ```

    If you run the game now, you will see the tile map that we just loaded and George and some of the enemies. You'll only see some of the enemies because some will be drawn offscreen. You will need to switch your emulator from portrait to landscape to see the map correctly.

In the next section, we are going to remove the hardcoded enemies and start using a map layer to add the enemies dynamically to the map.

Adding dynamic objects to the map

So far in the game, we have added a couple of each enemy, but now we are going to show you how enemies and other objects can be added dynamically to the game.

This is very common in games because you may want some treasure or an enemy to spawn at a certain location on the map. Tiled has a really great way to help us with this, with a feature called layers. The two most common layers are tile layers and object layers. We already used tile layers to display our map in the previous section, *Loading a tile map*. Object layers allow us to define objects that will be drawn on top of the map.

In the following screenshot, we show our tile map opened in Tiled, where you can see we have two layers named **Enemies** and **Map**. The **Map** layer is our tile layer, and the **Enemies** layer shows an object layer. We will use this **Enemies** layer to define spawn points for our enemies:

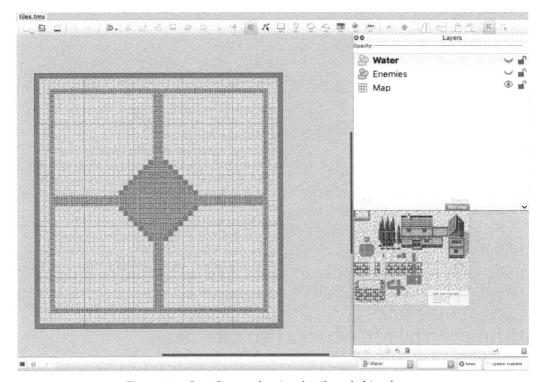

Figure 7.5 – Our tile map showing the tile and object layers

We have initially placed 12 enemies on the map, 3 enemies in each quadrant. The enemies will wander around as mentioned in the *Loading a tile map* section. When we have loaded them in the game, we will read their locations from the tile map object layer, **Enemies**. So, let's add them to our game next:

1. Open the main.dart file and remove the four lines where we previously added our enemies in our onLoad function:

    ```
    add (Zombie(position: Vector2(100, 200),
      size: Vector2(32.0, 64.0), speed: 20.0));
    add (Zombie(position: Vector2(300, 200),
      size: Vector2(32.0, 64.0), speed: 20.0));
    add (Skeleton(position: Vector2(100, 600),
    ```

```
  size: Vector2(32.0, 64.0), speed: 60.0));
add (Skeleton(position: Vector2(300, 600),
  size: Vector2(32.0, 64.0), speed: 60.0));
```

2. Add the following code to replace the code we just removed:

```
final enemies =
  tiledMap.tileMap.getObjectGroupFromLayer('Enemies');
enemies.objects.asMap().forEach((index, position) {
  if (index % 2 == 0) {
    add(Skeleton(position: Vector2(position.x,
      position.y), size: Vector2(32.0, 64.0),
        speed: 60.0));
  } else {
    add (Zombie(position: Vector2(position.x,
      position.y), size: Vector2(32.0, 64.0), speed:
        20.0));
  }
});
```

This code is to read the object layer from the tile map and iterate over the data, which contains 12 enemies, so that we place 6 skeletons and 6 zombies around the map.

If you run the game now, you will see that we have some enemies. However, you will currently see fewer of them because they are spread out around the map. Currently, we are only showing the top-left corner of the map, but before we learn to figure out how to move around the map in the *Understanding map navigation* section, let's add some other objects to the map.

If you recall from earlier in the book, in *Chapter 1, Getting Started with Flutter Games*, the final goal of the game is to collect gold coins to build up your score, but we don't yet have any gold coins in the game. So, let's fix that by introducing a new animated coin sprite and placing them in random locations all over the map. Of course, we could add these as an object layer on the tile map if we wanted to, but as we have seen how we can add fixed objects with the enemies, let's make the coins' locations random to make the game more fun.

3. Download the coins image from `https://github.com/PacktPublishing/` `Building-Games-with-Flutter/tree/main/chapter07/assets/` `images/coins.png` and save the image in our `assets/images` project folder.

4. Download the coin audio file from `https://github.com/` `PacktPublishing/Building-Games-with-Flutter/tree/main/` `chapter07/assets/audio/sounds/coin.wav` and save the audio file in our `assets/audio/sounds` project folder.

5. Open the `pubspec.yaml` file and add the following line to your list of assets:

   ```
   - assets/images/coins.png
   - assets/audio/sounds/coin.wav
   ```

6. Save the file and allow `pub get` to validate the asset:

   `flutter pub get`

7. In the `component` folder, create a file called `coin.dart` and open it. Then add the following class definition for the `Coin` class, which loads the coin image, creates an animation, and sets up the collision detection on the coin:

   ```dart
   import 'package:flame/components.dart';
   import 'package:flame/flame.dart';
   import 'package:flame/geometry.dart';
   import 'package:flame/sprite.dart';

   class Coin extends SpriteAnimationComponent with
     HasHitboxes, Collidable {
     Coin({required Vector2 position, required Vector2
       size}) : super(position: position, size: size);
     @override
     Future<void> onLoad() async {
       super.onLoad();

       var spriteImages =
         await Flame.images.load('coins.png');
       final spriteSheet =
         SpriteSheet(image: spriteImages, srcSize: size);
   ```

```
animation = spriteSheet.createAnimation(row: 0,
    stepTime: 0.1, from: 0, to: 7);

addHitbox(HitboxRectangle());
  }
}
```

8. Open the `main.dart` file and add the following imports at the top of the file:

    ```
    import 'package:goldrush/components/coin.dart';
    import 'dart:math';
    ```

9. In the `onLoad` function, add the following code below where we add the enemies; this will add the coins to the map:

    ```
    Random random =
      Random(DateTime.now().millisecondsSinceEpoch);
    for (int i = 0; i < 50; i++) {
      int randomX = random.nextInt(48) + 1;
      int randomY = random.nextInt(48) + 1;
      double posCoinX = (randomX * 32) + 5;
      double posCoinY = (randomY * 32) + 5;
      add(Coin(position: Vector2(posCoinX, posCoinY),
        size: Vector2(20, 20)));
    }
    ```

    The code creates a random number generator using the current clock time as the seed to initialize the random numbers, which will make the numbers truly random.

    If you want a more predictable sequence of numbers generated, you can pass the same fixed integer each time. This can be useful in games where you want to create a set of level data that's always the same but appears to be random.

    Next, we generate a number between 1 and 48, because we don't want to draw coins on the water tiles. Later, we will add collision detection to the water tiles to prevent the player or enemies from walking on the water. By generating a number with these bounds, it will give us a location on the map related to the map array data.

    We then take those numbers and multiply the number by 32, which is the size of the map tile, and add 5 to get the `posCoinX` and `posCoinY` values, which is the location of the coin in pixels.

We then use these values to add a new coin component to the map at this position.

Note that we do all this in a loop that adds 50 coins to the map, some of which will be currently offscreen until we add the map navigation.

10. Now that we have our coins added to the map, let's continue and update the `George` class so that George can collect the coins.

11. Open the `george.dart` file and at the top of the file, add the following import:

```
import 'package:goldrush/components/coin.dart';
```

12. At the bottom of the `onLoad` function, update the line that loads the audio files into the audio cache to load the `coin.wav` audio file:

```
await FlameAudio.audioCache.loadAll(
  ['sounds/enemy_dies.wav', 'sounds/running.wav',
   'sounds/coin.wav']);
```

13. Finally, at the bottom of the `onCollision` function, let's add a check for a collision with a coin – if we collide with a coin, it will remove the coin from the game, update our score by 20, and play the coin audio:

```
if (other is Coin) {
  other.removeFromParent();
  hud.scoreText.setScore(20);
  FlameAudio.play('sounds/coin.wav', volume: 1.0);
}
```

If you run the game now, you will see the spinning coins on the map and you will be able to move George around a little to collect the coins. However, you will notice that we are still constrained to the top-left corner of the map, even if we try to move beyond this top corner.

In the next section, we will break George and the enemies free of this restriction, allowing them to move around the map by adding navigation to the game map!

Understanding map navigation

Now that we have our tile map loaded and enemies and coins dynamically added to the map, we can fix the navigation so we can wander around the map. But before we do that, let's talk about cameras and how we use them in our game.

A camera allows us to change what we see on the screen, which is very useful when you have a map that is larger than the physical screen. We can use this to do the following:

- Zoom the camera to show more or less of the map.

- Show a different part of the map than George's current location on the map.

- Move to a different part of the map using animation for a smooth transition.

- Link the camera's position to follow George, so that when George moves around the map, the camera updates and George stays visible, and the map moves around his position.

Most games use a combination of these, but it is the last point we are most interested in, as we want the camera to follow George as he moves around.

> **Important Note**
>
> Look up cameras in the Flame documentation if you are interested in learning more about the other points. The documentation for cameras can be found at `https://docs.flame-engine.org/main/camera_and_viewport.html`.

Let's get started with fixing the navigation:

1. Open the `main.dart` file and at the bottom on the `onLoad` function, add the following code:

```
camera.speed = 1;
camera.followComponent(george, worldBounds:
  Rect.fromLTWH(0, 0, 1600, 1600));
```

Here, we set the camera speed, set the camera to follow George, and set the bounds of the world to be 1,600 x 1,600, which is the 50 tiles' width and height times the pixel size of each tile, which is 32.

If you run this now and navigate around the map, you may notice a couple of issues:

a. The enemies don't wander any further than the original screen size.

b. You can only touch to move within the original screen size.

Let's fix each of these issues in turn.

2. The reason why the enemies don't move around the map is that they are colliding with the `ScreenCollidable` that we added when the screen was a fixed size. As we will do the collision for this in the next section, we can just delete the line where we added the `ScreenCollidable` file at the bottom of the `onLoad` function:

    ```
    add(ScreenCollidable());
    ```

3. The reason why you can only touch within the physical screen bounds is that the touch events are picked up in the `Background` class, and the `Background` class size is currently based on the physical dimensions of the screen.

    Also, now, as we are drawing the map, the background is only used to detect and pass on the touch event to George, so we can remove most of the drawing code from the `Background` class. Open the `background.dart` file and change all the code in the class and add the reduced code, as follows:

    ```dart
    import 'package:flame/components.dart';
    import 'package:flame/input.dart';
    import 'george.dart';

    class Background extends PositionComponent with
      Tappable {

      Background(this.george);

      final George george;

      @override
      Future<void> onLoad() async {
        super.onLoad();

        position = Vector2(0, 0);
        size = Vector2(1600, 1600);
      }

      @override
      bool onTapUp(TapUpInfo info) {
        george.moveToLocation(info);
    ```

```
        return true;
    }
}
```

Apart from reducing the code in this class, the main change is at the bottom of the onLoad function, where we set the size to 1,600 x 1,600, which is the map size and not the screen size that we had previously in the *Drawing onscreen controls* section of *Chapter 5*, *Moving the Graphics with Input*.

If you run the game now, you will see these issues are fixed and we can navigate around and collect coins. Unfortunately, now that we have removed ScreenCollidable, George and the enemies can walk off the sides of the screen.

In the next section, we will fix this by making the water around the map into a collidable object that we can check for as we move around the map, detecting whether we collide with the water and preventing George or the enemies from moving over it.

Detecting tile collisions

So far in our game, we have used component-level collision detection to detect collisions between George and the coins and enemies. When you are working with map levels, you will generally add other objects on the map that act as barriers, such as water, buildings, or trees. As the player navigates around maps with these types of items, we want to ensure that neither George nor enemies walk through these objects.

In the *Understanding map navigation* section, we removed the ScreenCollidable component to allow the enemies to freely move around the map, but now the enemies and George can wander off the map.

In this section, we are going to add a water barrier that will go around the map. We will check for collisions to prevent both George and the enemies from being able to leave the map. We will read the map locations of the water from an object layer and create new Water components. We will make these components collidable and add these to the game so that Flame will check for collisions with the water and we can prevent George or the enemies from moving over the water.

This presents some interesting challenges because with our previous collision checks, we just remove the enemy or coin when George collides with them, and George can continue to move in the direction he is traveling in, but now we will have to prevent movement when we collide with the water. Before we get into that, let's first talk a little bit more about what is happening when Flame checks for collisions.

Understanding collisions

When we set up a component to be collidable, we are adding a shape around the object. Then, Flame can use these shapes to calculate if one shape intersects with another shape and trigger a collision detection if that happens.

As the game grows, we keep adding more items that can be collided with, and the problem with this process is that for every collidable item we add to the game, there needs to be a collision check. The more collision checks we have, the more effort is required by the processor to handle all the math behind that. Eventually, if you have too many collision checks, the performance of the game will degrade, and you will notice that the game starts to slow down.

Let's look at some of the math that we have in the game so far, to put this in context:

- We have 12 enemies in the game, 6 zombies and 6 skeletons.

- We have 50 coins in the game.

- We are going to add borders around the edges of the map, so that could be around 200 water components due to each edge having 50 tiles with 4 edges around the map.

- We also have our player, George.

This is 263 collidable objects in the game. At the moment, every one of these collidable objects has a collision check with every other collidable object in the game. So, that is 263 * 263 = 69,169 collision checks. That's nearly 70,000 collision checks, and that's happening every frame!

That's a scary number of collision checks and it's surprising our game is still running!

If you think about it, most of those checks are a complete waste, because a coin cannot collide with other coins as they are all spread out around the map, and they don't move. This is the same for the water objects that we will add too. Also, the water objects can't collide with the coins either as they are in different locations.

Fortunately, Flame provides a great solution to this issue by allowing us to set `collidableType` on the collidable component to let us tell Flame whether we should do a check or not for this object.

The three collidable types are as follows:

- **Active**: An active collidable collides with other collidable objects that are of the active or passive type. This is the default collidable type, if you don't set the value for all collidable objects.

- **Passive**: A passive collidable collides with other collidables of the active type but not with other passive collidable objects.

- **Inactive**: An inactive collidable will not collide with other collidable objects.

The solution for us to reduce the number of collision checks is to make the `Water` and `Coin` objects passive and leave George and the enemy objects in their default active state.

Implementing collisions

Let's get started by adding the `Water` objects to our game:

1. In the project's `component` folder, create a new file called `water.dart` and add the following code:

    ```
    import 'package:flame/components.dart';
    import 'package:flame/geometry.dart';

    class Water extends PositionComponent with
      HasHitboxes, Collidable {

      Water({required Vector2 position, required Vector2
        size, required this.id}) : super(position:
          position, size: size);

      int id;

      @override
      Future<void> onLoad() async {
        super.onLoad();

        collidableType = CollidableType.passive;

        addHitbox(HitboxRectangle());
      }
    }
    ```

    Here, we define the `Water` object, which is a rectangular area that has a position and size.

In the onLoad function, we set collidableType to be of the CollidableType.passive type and add a hitbox for the collision checks between George and Water and the enemies and Water.

2. Open the main.dart file and at the bottom of the onLoad function, add the following code below where we added the coins:

```
final water =
  tiledMap.tileMap.getObjectGroupFromLayer('Water');
water.objects.forEach((rect) {
  add(Water(position: Vector2(rect.x, rect.y), size:
    Vector2(rect.width, rect.height), id: rect.id));
});
```

Here, we get the water objects from the tile map as an object group and iterate over these objects, using the x, y, width, and height values from this to create and add a Water component to the game.

If you open the tile map in Tiled, you can see that the Water object layer consists of four simple rectangles, which reduces the amount of collisions checks. We don't really care about which individual water tile we collide with, so we can just check the four edges.

3. At the top of the same file, add the following import for the Water component:

```
import 'package:goldrush/components/water.dart';
```

4. Open the coin.dart file and add the following code to the onLoad function to set collidableType to be passive:

```
super.onLoad();
collidableType = CollidableType.passive;
```

5. Let's change the collision for the enemies first as it's a very quick change. Open the character_enemy.dart file and at the top of the onCollision function, let's change the object check to use the Water object instead of ScreenCollidable with the following code:

```
if (other is Water) {
```

6. Next, we need to add the import for the Water class at the top of this file:

```
import 'package:goldrush/components/water.dart';
```

Moving on, Flame has debugMode, which we can set to true to see the bounding boxes (a box that shows the boundary limits of the area of detection) of the collidable boxes, which is useful for debugging collision detection. Let's add that next.

7. Open the main.dart file and at the top of the onLoad function, add the following line:

```
debugMode = true;
```

If you run the game now, you will see the bounding boxes and you may notice an issue.

The Skeleton and Zombie sprites have a large amount of space at the top of the sprites, which means if George collides with the top of these sprites, the collision will happen sooner than expected because of the extra space in the image. To get around this, we can pass two values to HitboxRectangle, which are relation and relativeOffset.

The relation value defines the relationship between the length of the horizontal and vertical sides and the size of the bounding box, and the relativeOffset value is the position of your shape in relation to its size from (-1,-1) to (1,1).

To fix the space issue at the top of the enemy sprite classes, open both the zombie. dart and skeleton.dart files, and at the bottom of the onLoad function, change the line that adds the hitbox in both classes to the following code:

```
addHitbox(HitboxRectangle(relation: Vector2(1.0, 0.7))..
relativeOffset = Vector2(0.0, 0.3));
```

If you run the game now, you will see the bounding box is tightly aligned with the size of the sprite, which will give us much better results with the collision detection.

8. We can also tweak the sprite that we use for George to improve the bounding box further on the George sprite. Open the george.dart file and at the bottom of the onLoad function, change the line that adds the hitbox to the following code:

```
addHitbox(HitboxRectangle(relation: Vector2(0.7, 0.7))..
relativeOffset = Vector2(0.0, 0.1));
```

Please note that the values are different from the ones we used for the enemy sprites.

9. Now that we have finished tweaking our bounding boxes, we can now remove the debugMode line in the main.dart file.

10. Let's continue adding the final collision checks in the `George` class.

At the top of the `George` class where we previously defined the class variables, add these two new variables, which we will use to keep track of whether we have collided with the `Water` component and what the direction of travel was when we collided:

```
int collisionDirection = Character.down;
bool hasCollided = false;
```

We set `collisionDirection` to down because George starts the game facing down.

11. Next, let's add an import for the `Water` object, which we are going to use in the collision check. At the top of the file where the rest of the imports are, add the following import:

```
import 'package:goldrush/components/water.dart';
```

12. At the bottom of the `onCollision` function, let's add the following code to set the collision variables when a collision is detected with the `Water` border:

```
if (other is Water) {
  if (!hasCollided) {
    if (movingToTouchedLocation) {
        movingToTouchedLocation = false;
    } else {
      hasCollided = true;
      collisionDirection = currentDirection;
    }
  }
}
```

We will use these values in the next few steps to prevent us from moving George when we collide with the water. But also notice in the preceding code that if a collision has been detected and we are moving to a touched location, we now set `movingToTouchedLocation` to `false` to stop George from continuing to try to move.

13. We also want to set the `hasCollided` variable back to `false` when a collision has ended, and fortunately Flame has a function called `onCollisionEnd` that we can override and will get called when the objects have stopped colliding:

```
@override
void onCollisionEnd(Collidable other) {
  hasCollided = false;
}
```

14. Next, we will create a function for handling all our movement code and will only allow the movement if there hasn't been a collision. Because we calculate the movement of a touched location differently, we will split the code up based on whether we are moving to a touched location or not, or whether the player is using the joystick to control the movement:

```
void movePlayer(double delta) {
  if (!(hasCollided && collisionDirection ==
    currentDirection)) {
    if (movingToTouchedLocation) {
      position.add((targetLocation -
        position).normalized() * (speed * delta));
    } else {
      switch (currentDirection) {
        case Character.left:
          position.add(Vector2(delta * -speed, 0));
        break;
        case Character.right:
          position.add(Vector2(delta * speed, 0));
        break;
        case Character.up:
          position.add(Vector2(0, delta * -speed));
        break;
        case Character.down:
          position.add(Vector2(0, delta * speed));
        break;
      }
    }
  }
}
```

15. Let's update the `update` function and replace the two places where we change the sprite position for both touch and joystick control.

Replace the following line with `movePlayer(dt);`:

```
position.add(hud.joystick.relativeDelta * speed * dt);
```

Also, replace the following line with `movePlayer(dt);`:

```
position += (targetLocation - position).normalized() *
(speed * dt);
```

If you run the app now and move around with the joystick or by touch, you will see that you can't go outside of the screen, as we now collide with the water and prevent the player from moving over the water and outside the bounds of the screen.

Summary

In this chapter, we learned all about tile maps, how to create them and add dynamic objects, and how to navigate around them while avoiding colliding with our collision objects.

So far in the book, we have mainly been building the game for mobile, but Flutter also supports other platforms. In the next chapter, we will show you how to build the app for web and desktop, convert the game to support the bigger available screen area, and add extra controls to move George around with the keyboard.

Questions

1. What is the Tiled application used for?

2. Why should we use a tile map instead of one large image for the map?

3. How is map data stored inside a tile map?

4. What are the different types of layers that we can use on our tile maps?

5. How can we use a camera to adjust the map to keep a sprite in focus while we navigate around the map?

6. How can we add collidable objects using tile maps?

7. What are the three collidable types and why are they needed?

8
Scaling the Game for Web and Desktop

So far in this book, we have focused on building games for mobile devices that have small fixed-size screens. One of the benefits of Flutter, of course, is that it is a cross-platform framework that works on mobile, the web, and desktop.

However, when building a game that will run on a website, there are issues that we don't face on mobile. If, instead of launching one of the mobile emulators, you choose the Chrome browser as the target platform in Visual Studio Code and then run the game, you would notice that the map and UI are drawn incorrectly, that there is no background music, and touch events don't work properly.

In this chapter, we will convert the game so that it works on the web and desktop, making sure to fix these issues. When dealing with resizing, we will need to redraw the map and reposition all our components based on our new screen size. Some screens are very high resolution and larger than our physical map size of 1,600 x 1,600, which means we will need to ensure our game still looks great on these larger screens.

In this chapter, we will cover the following topics:

- Building the game for the web and desktop
- Setting background music
- Setting Flutter Web build parameters
- Navigating with key events

Technical requirements

To examine the source from this chapter, you can download it from `https://github.com/PacktPublishing/Building-Games-with-Flutter/tree/main/chapter08`.

Building the game for the web and desktop

As mentioned in the introduction, if you launched our game in Google Chrome, you would notice that the map and UI are drawn incorrectly and are in the wrong places. So, what is going on here?

The larger screen size that is changing constantly when we resize the screen is confusing our game, which currently thinks the size is fixed and the initial positions of our components are set relative to our fixed screen size. Because of this confusion, the graphics can look weird and our previously working touch events can now get confused because of this new screen size.

The solution to this is to ask the game to tell us when the screen is resized, and for us to use the new screen size to recalculate the positions of all our components. To make this more straightforward, we are going to mathematically calculate the boundaries of our game so that we know where the top, left, right, and bottom of our map are in relation to our new screen size, and then adjust the components based on this boundary.

The following image shows what we want to achieve by fixing the current user interface issues:

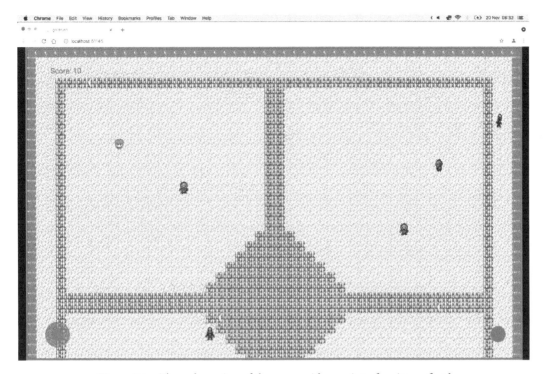

Figure 8.1 – The web version of the game with user interface issues fixed

In *Figure 8.1*, you can see that when the screen is wider than the map, the tile component draws black borders for the empty space. As the screen's width is larger than the map's width, we see these black borders on the sides, but this is not the case for the height. The screen's height is less than the map's height, so no black borders are drawn at the top and bottom. This may be different on your screen depending on your screen size.

The red rectangle in the preceding image shows the boundary that we want to calculate so that we can adjust everything else relative to it. In this section, we will do just that.

Setting the new screen boundary

Now that we know the boundary we need to calculate, let's go ahead and add it to our code:

1. Open the `maths_utils.dart` file and add the following function:

    ```
    Rect getGameScreenBounds(Vector2 canvasSize) {
    }
    ```

2. At the top of the `getGameScreenBounds` function, add this code:

    ```
    double left = 0, right = 0, top = 0, bottom = 0;

    if (canvasSize.x > 1600) {
      left = (canvasSize.x - 1600) / 2;
    }
    if (canvasSize.y > 1600) {
      top = (canvasSize.y - 1600) / 2;
    }
    ```

    Here, we initially define some variables to store our `left`, `right`, `top`, and `bottom` values.

    If the width or height of the screen is less than the map size, 1,600 x 1,600, we set the default values to `0, 0` and only update the default values if the width or height of the screen is greater than the map size.

    We pass in `canvasSize` to the function, which is the current screen size, and deduct `1600` to get the total difference between the two values. We then divide the total difference by 2 because we want to ensure any adjustments will center the map in the available space.

    We will call this function at the start of the game, and every time the player changes the screen size by resizing the window, we will then adjust all the components based on this new screen size so they look correct.

3. Let's continue in our `getGameScreenBounds` function and set our `right` and `top` variables next:

    ```
    if (canvasSize.x < 1600) {
      right = canvasSize.x;
    } else {
      right = left + 1600;
    ```

```
}

if (canvasSize.y < 1600) {
  bottom = canvasSize.y;
} else {
  bottom = top + 1600;
}

return Rect.fromLTRB(left, top, right, bottom);
```

Here, we check whether the screen's width is less than `1600`, and if it is, we set the `right` value to the screen's width. Otherwise, to get the `right` value, we add the `left` value and the map's width, `1600`.

Then we do the same calculation for the `bottom` value using the screen's height instead.

Next, we create a rectangle to store our values and return it from the function.

> **Important Note**
> All the values are based on the absolute pixel values to help us when we calculate the positions of the components, and especially the HUD, which must align closely with the corners.

4. Finally, we add the following `import` at the top of the file to resolve the references to the `Vector2` and `Rect` classes we use in this function:

```
import 'package:flame/extensions.dart';
```

Now that we have the maths sorted for calculating the bounds when the screen resizes, let's start applying this to our components.

Fixing the sprites

We will start with George and the enemies, which have a top-level base class of `Character`. So, let's listen for the game resize event in that class:

1. Open the `character.dart` file and add the following variable to the `Character` class to keep track of the original position of the sprite:

```
late Vector2 originalPosition;
```

2. Next, let's add the code to listen for the game resize event by overriding the onGameResize function that is part of the Component class, which all our sprites inherit from. Then we adjust the current position based on originalPosition and the current game screen bounds, as shown here:

```
@override
void onGameResize(Vector2 canvasSize) {
super.onGameResize(canvasSize);

Rect gameScreenBounds =
  getGameScreenBounds(canvasSize);
position = Vector2(originalPosition.x +
  gameScreenBounds.left, originalPosition.y +
    gameScreenBounds.top);
}
```

3. Now that we have the code for handling the resizing, let's add the imports at the top of this file:

```
import 'package:goldrush/utils/math_utils.dart';
import 'package:flame/extensions.dart';
```

With the Character base class resizing now handled, it's very easy to fix George and the enemies. We just need to store the original position in the constructor and the sprites will move correctly when the screen is resized by their callback to onGameResize, which is handled in their Character base class.

4. So, open the george.dart file and change the constructor to this:

```
George({required this.hud, required Vector2 position,
  required Vector2 size, required double speed}) :
    super(position: position, size: size, speed:
      speed) {
    originalPosition = position;
  }
```

5. Next, open the skeleton.dart file and change the constructor to this:

```
Skeleton({required Vector2 position, required Vector2
  size, required double speed}) : super(position:
    position, size: size, speed: speed) {
```

```
      originalPosition = position;
    }
```

6. Then, open the `zombie.dart` file and change the constructor to this:

```
Zombie({required Vector2 position, required Vector2
  size, required double speed}) : super(position:
    position, size: size, speed: speed) {
  originalPosition = position;
}
```

Now that we have fixed our main sprites, let's fix the `Coin` and `Water` components.

Fixing the coin and water components

To start fixing the water and coin components, perform the following steps:

1. Open the `coin.dart` file, change the `Coin` class constructor, and add a variable for the original position like this:

```
Coin({required Vector2 position, required Vector2
  size}) :
  originalPosition = position,
  super(position: position, size: size);


late Vector2 originalPosition;
```

2. Add the following `onGameResize` function to the `Coin` class:

```
@override
void onGameResize(Vector2 canvasSize) {
  super.onGameResize(canvasSize);
  Rect gameScreenBounds =
    getGameScreenBounds(canvasSize);
  position = Vector2(originalPosition.x +
    gameScreenBounds.left, originalPosition.y +
      gameScreenBounds.top);
}
```

3. And finally for the Coin class, let's add the imports at the top of the file:

    ```
    import 'dart:ui';
    import 'package:goldrush/utils/math _ utils.dart';
    ```

    The code we have added to the Coin class is similar to what we added to the Character classes where we store the originalPosition in the constructor, and then use this value with the new screen size when the game gets resized to calculate our new position.

    Let's do the same for the Water class.

4. Open the water.dart file, change the Water class constructor, and add a variable for the original position like this:

    ```
    Water({required Vector2 position, required Vector2
      size, required this.id}) :
      originalPosition = position,
      super(position: position, size: size);


    late Vector2 originalPosition;
    ```

5. Add the following onGameResize function to the Water class:

    ```
    @override
    void onGameResize(Vector2 canvasSize) {
      super.onGameResize(canvasSize);
      Rect gameScreenBounds =
        getGameScreenBounds(canvasSize);
      position = Vector2(originalPosition.x +
        gameScreenBounds.left, originalPosition.y +
          gameScreenBounds.top);
    }
    ```

6. And finally for the Water class, let's add the imports at the top of the file:

    ```
    import 'package:goldrush/utils/math _ utils.dart';
    import 'dart:ui';
    ```

Now that we have fixed the sprites, let's fix the background and the tile map.

Fixing the background and tile map

For our tile map, we currently use TiledComponent, which itself extends from the Component class. This is the base class for all other components, and this class doesn't itself have a position. This is a problem for tracking the game bounds for the tile map. So, the solution for this is to wrap our TiledComponent around another class, which we will name TileMapComponent.

TileMapComponent is itself a position component and we will make TiledComponent a child of the new TileMapComponent class. By doing this, we can freely position this new class when the screen resizes.

So, let's continue and add this new wrapper class:

1. In the components folder, create a new file called tilemap.dart and add the following code:

    ```dart
    import 'package:flame/components.dart';
    import 'package:flame_tiled/flame_tiled.dart';
    import 'package:flutter/material.dart';
    import 'package:goldrush/utils/math_utils.dart';

    class TileMapComponent extends PositionComponent {

      TileMapComponent(this.tiledComponent) {
        add(tiledComponent);
      }

      TiledComponent tiledComponent;

      @override
      void onGameResize(Vector2 canvasSize) {
        super.onGameResize(canvasSize);

        Rect gameScreenBounds =
          getGameScreenBounds(canvasSize);
        if (canvasSize.x > 1600) {
          double xAdjust = (canvasSize.x - 1600) / 2;
          position = Vector2(gameScreenBounds.left +
            xAdjust, gameScreenBounds.top);
    ```

```
      } else {
        position = Vector2(gameScreenBounds.left,
          gameScreenBounds.top);
      }
      size = Vector2(1600, 1600);
    }
  }
```

In this new class, we take `TiledComponent` via the constructor and add it as a child component, so it will be positioned in the same position as this class. Then, in the `onGameResize` function, we are adjusting the position and fixing the size of this component to the map size, 1,600 x 1,600.

Moving on to the `Background` class, in this class, we want to remove the `position` and `size` settings – that happens currently in the `onLoad` function – by removing this function and then setting `position` and `size` in the `onGameResize` function.

2. Open the `background.dart` file, remove the `onLoad` function completely, and add the following code:

```
@override
void onGameResize(Vector2 canvasSize) {
  super.onGameResize(canvasSize);

  Rect gameScreenBounds =
    getGameScreenBounds(canvasSize);
  if (canvasSize.x > 1600) {
    double xAdjust = (canvasSize.x - 1600) / 2;
    position = Vector2(gameScreenBounds.left +
      xAdjust, gameScreenBounds.top);
  } else {
    position = Vector2(gameScreenBounds.left,
      gameScreenBounds.top);
  }
  size = Vector2(1600, 1600);
}
```

As with the `TileMapComponent` object we just added, this sets `position` and `size` based on the new screen size, after a resize.

> **Important Note**
>
> Please note that `onGameResize` is always called when the component is first created and then again any time after that if the screen is resized. Therefore, we don't need to do anything on `onLoad` anymore.

3. Next, let's add the imports:

    ```
    import 'package:goldrush/utils/math_utils.dart';
    import 'dart:ui';
    ```

4. Finally for the `Background` class, we are going to change the constructor to increase the `priority` of the component to ensure that touch events are being picked up currently. Please change the constructor to the following:

    ```
    Background(this.george) : super(priority: 20);
    ```

In the next section, we will discuss how to fix the HUD components.

Fixing the HUD components

Now let's move on to fixing the HUD components.

Currently, in our HUD, we use the margins to adjust the joystick, run button, and score text locations based on the corners of the screen. There are some known issues at present with the Flame library when the game screen resizes that prevent this from working correctly.

So, we will rewrite part of the HUD to use position instead of margins, and then we can apply our usual calculations of getting the game screen bounds and adjusting the position of the HUD components when the screen resizes.

As in *step 2* of the *Fixing the background and tile map* section, with the `Background` class, we are going to remove the `onLoad` functionality and do the resizing in the `onGameResize` function. We are also going to split this function in two. The first time `onGameResize` is called, we need to create the HUD components and add them as children adjusting their positions based on the screen size. Every time after that when `onGameResize` is called, we will just update the HUD components' new positions.

To keep track of this, we will create a variable called isInitialised to track whether we have set up the HUD components already and call the correct code based on that:

1. Open the hud.dart file and add the isInitialised variable at the top of the class:

    ```
    bool isInitialised = false;
    ```

2. Remove the onLoad function and add the following code:

    ```
    @override
    void onGameResize(Vector2 canvasSize) {
      super.onGameResize(canvasSize);

      Rect gameScreenBounds =
        getGameScreenBounds(canvasSize);

      if(!isInitialised) {
      } else {
      }
    }
    ```

3. In the first if code block that checks whether isInitialised is false, add the following code:

    ```
    final joystickKnobPaint =
      BasicPalette.blue.withAlpha(200).paint();
    final joystickBackgroundPaint =
      BasicPalette.blue.withAlpha(100).paint();
    final buttonRunPaint =
      BasicPalette.red.withAlpha(200).paint();
    final buttonDownRunPaint =
      BasicPalette.red.withAlpha(100).paint();

    joystick = Joystick(
    knob: CircleComponent(radius: 20.0, paint:
      joystickKnobPaint),
    background: CircleComponent(radius: 40.0, paint:
      joystickBackgroundPaint),
    ```

```
  position: Vector2(gameScreenBounds.left + 100,
    gameScreenBounds.bottom - 80),
);
runButton = RunButton(
button: CircleComponent(radius: 25.0, paint:
  buttonRunPaint),
buttonDown: CircleComponent(radius: 25.0, paint:
  buttonDownRunPaint),
position: Vector2(gameScreenBounds.right - 80,
  gameScreenBounds.bottom - 80),
onPressed: () => {}
);
scoreText = ScoreText(position: Vector2(
  gameScreenBounds.left + 80, gameScreenBounds.top +
    60));
add(joystick);
add(runButton);
add(scoreText);
positionType = PositionType.viewport;
isInitialised = true;
```

Most of this code will be familiar from our previous `onLoad` function. Then we set up our HUD components using `position` instead of margins and add them as children. And then set the `isInitialised` variable to `true`, so we don't rerun this code every time the game is resized and keep on adding more components.

You may notice at this point that the child components show an error as they don't currently have a `position` value, but we will fix that soon.

4. In the `else` block, please add the following code, which will update the position of components that we created in the `if` block:

```
joystick.position = Vector2(gameScreenBounds.left +
  80, gameScreenBounds.bottom - 80);
runButton.position = Vector2(gameScreenBounds.right -
  80, gameScreenBounds.bottom - 80);
scoreText.position = Vector2(gameScreenBounds.left +
  80, gameScreenBounds.top + 60);
```

5. And finally, for the HudComponent class, let's add the imports at the top of the file:

    ```
    import 'package:goldrush/utils/math_utils.dart';
    ```

    Next, let's fix the Joystick and ScoreText classes to use positions instead of margin. Note the RunButton class already had the position value in its constructor, so we don't need to update the RunButton class.

6. Open the joystick.dart file and change the constructor to the following:

    ```
    Joystick({required PositionComponent knob,
        PositionComponent? background, Vector2? position}) :
          super (knob: knob, background: background,
            position: position);
    ```

7. We can also now remove the unused import:

    ```
    import 'package:flutter/material.dart';
    ```

8. Open the score_text.dart file and change the constructor to the following:

    ```
    ScoreText({Vector2? position}) : super (position:
        position);
    ```

    Now let's switch our focus to tying up all these component changes by making changes in our main.dart file to use the new game screen bounds.

9. Open the main.dart file and add the following imports at the top of the file:

    ```
    import 'package:goldrush/components/tilemap.dart';
    import 'package:goldrush/utils/math_utils.dart';
    ```

    In the onLoad function, we want to set up the originalPosition variables for each component by calculating the game screen bounds and using the result from this along with our intended position to adjust the position when the screen is resized.

10. Continuing in the main.dart file, let's add the code to get the game screen bounds below where we call onLoad in the base class:

    ```
    @override
    Future<void> onLoad() async {
      super.onLoad();
    ```

```
Rect gameScreenBounds =
   getGameScreenBounds(canvasSize);
```

11. Next, let's update where we create the `George` class by passing the `position`. Let's also change the `priority` of the `George` component to fix a loading issue that only happens on the web:

```
var george = George(hud: hud, position:
   Vector2(gameScreenBounds.left + 300,
      gameScreenBounds.top + 300), size: Vector2(48.0,
         48.0), speed: 40.0);
add (george);
children.changePriority(george, 15);
```

12. Where we create and load the `TiledComponent` data, we now need to wrap it with our new `TileMapComponent`:

```
final tiledMap = await
   TiledComponent.load('tiles.tmx', Vector2.all(32));
add(TileMapComponent(tiledMap));
```

13. Let's change the positions of the `Skeleton` and `Zombie` classes next:

```
if (index % 2 == 0) {
   add(Skeleton(position: Vector2(position.x +
      gameScreenBounds.left, position.y +
         gameScreenBounds.top), size: Vector2(32.0,
            64.0), speed: 60.0));
} else {
   add(Zombie(position: Vector2(position.x +
      gameScreenBounds.left, position.y +
         gameScreenBounds.top), size: Vector2(32.0,
            64.0), speed: 20.0));
}
```

14. Next, let's fix the `Coin` class with the new `position`:

```
double posCoinX = (randomX * 32) + 5 + gameScreenBounds.
left;
double posCoinY = (randomY * 32) + 5 + gameScreenBounds.
top;
```

15. And next, let's fix the `Water` class' `position`:

```
add(Water(position: Vector2(rect.x +
  gameScreenBounds.left, rect.y +
    gameScreenBounds.top), size: Vector2(rect.width,
      rect.height), id: rect.id));
```

16. And finally for the user interface issues, let's update the camera so that when it follows `George`, it considers the new game screen bounds:

```
camera.followComponent(george, worldBounds:
  Rect.fromLTWH(gameScreenBounds.left,
    gameScreenBounds.top, 1600, 1600));
```

If you have not previously set up the app for the web, you may need to run the following command in the project folder to create the web folder for the project: `flutter create`.

> **Note**
> All these changes will modify the existing lines in place and use the new game screen bounds along with an initial position where needed.

Now that we have fixed the user interface issues, let's look at why the music isn't playing in the background.

Setting background music

Modern browsers such as Chrome, Safari, and Firefox block websites from playing audio in the background until the user has interacted with the page to ensure that this is what the user really wants. Websites often open pop up sites that annoy users with advertisements. So, the companies that make these browsers added measures such as preventing background audio to give the user more control over these annoying popups.

The browsers specifically don't want background music attempting to play when a page is first loaded, which we are trying to do by starting the music in our game's `onLoad` function. To fix this for our game temporarily, we can click on the padlock icon that is to the left of the website address and enable any sound permissions in Chrome. Then refresh the page and you will hear the background music again.

Figure 8.2 – Audio permissions in the Chrome browser

This is fine for development, but obviously not great for your players who may visit your website. In the final chapter, *Chapter 11, Finishing the Game*, we will add some setting screens to the game and allow the player to turn on background music based on a user interface interaction. This will allow the user to turn the music on or off, based on the player's preferences.

In the next section, we will discuss build parameters that we can set to improve the performance of Flutter Web.

Setting Flutter Web build parameters

If you run the game now using Chrome as the device, you will see you can resize the browser window and the page will resize, and components will be updated based on this, although when running the game, the performance isn't great. So, let's discuss how we compile the code for a release and deploy it via a web server for better performance.

When building a web release, we must pass a parameter to the `flutter build web` command to indicate the web renderer we want to choose from these two options:

- `html`: Choose this web renderer if you are optimizing download size over performance.
- `canvaskit`: Choose this web renderer if you are prioritizing performance and pixel-perfect consistency across platforms.

We will use `canvaskit` as performance is more important than download size nowadays, but just be aware that `html` is there as an option if you ever need it:

1. Let's run the command that will create our release build.

    Open a command-line terminal in the project folder and type the following:

    ```
    flutter build web --release --web-renderer canvaskit
    ```

    When this has finished compiling, it will save the web code in the `build/web` folder.

2. Next, let's run the web server from the `build/web` folder:

    ```
    cd build/web/
    python3 -m http.server 8000 &
    ```

    Here, we move to the folder where the web code is and run the web server.

    We are using the build in web server that the Python language provides for free.

    If you don't have Python installed, please go online and install it from `https://www.python.org/downloads/` before running this command.

    If you have your own web host, you can also upload the contents of the `build/web` folder to your web host.

3. With the web server running our game, open any browser and enter `http://localhost:8000/` in the browser's address bar.

    The game will load, and you will see it running in your browser. You will also notice it loads and runs a lot faster than running it via the Chrome device.

    When you have finished playing the game on the web, you should shut down the web server. Because the web server is running in the background, we need to bring it to the foreground first to shut it down.

4. In your terminal, press the *Enter* key to start a new line and then type the following to bring the web server to the foreground:

   ```
   fg
   ```

5. Next, hit the keys *Ctrl + C* to stop the web server.

If you need to start and stop the web server as you add new pieces of code that you want to test, please be aware of a couple of things:

- You should always compile a release build from the project folder.
- You should always run the web server from the `build/web` folder.

In this section, we addressed the issues with dynamically sized user interfaces and discussed a workaround for the background audio issue. We also discussed how to create a release build for the web and tested this on a web server.

In the next section, we will discuss how to navigate with physical keys.

Navigating with key events

Our game already allows the player character to be controlled with either the joystick or touch events, but for websites, a more common method would be to use the keyboard to control the character.

In this section, we will add keyboard control as another option, so let's get started.

To listen for keyboard events in the game, we first have to tell our game that some of our components will listen for keyboard events:

1. Open the `main.dart` file and change the class definition to include the `HasKeyboardHandlerComponents` mixin:

   ```
   class GoldRush extends FlameGame with HasCollidables,
     HasDraggables, HasTappables,
       HasKeyboardHandlerComponents {
   ```

2. Add the following input import at the top of the same file:

   ```
   import 'package:flame/input.dart';
   ```

3. Open the `george.dart` file where we will listen for keyboard events and change the class definition to add the `KeyboardHandler` mixin:

```
class George extends Character with KeyboardHandler {
```

4. Add the following import at the top of the same file:

```
import 'package:flutter/services.dart';
```

5. Next, let's add some variables to store the state of the keys that are pressed:

```
bool keyLeftPressed = false, keyRightPressed = false,
  keyUpPressed = false, keyDownPressed = false,
    keyRunningPressed = false;
```

In our game, we will use the following key mappings:

a. Left = *A* key

b. Right = *D* key

c. Up = *W* key

d. Down = *S* key

e. Run = *R* key

6. Override the following function to the `George` class to listen for key events and set the variable set up in *step 5* correctly, if any of the keys are pressed:

```
@override
bool onKeyEvent(RawKeyEvent event,
  Set<LogicalKeyboardKey> keysPressed) {
  if (event.data.keyLabel.toLowerCase().contains('a'))
    { keyLeftPressed = (event is RawKeyDownEvent); }
  if (event.data.keyLabel.toLowerCase().contains('d'))
    { keyRightPressed = (event is RawKeyDownEvent); }
  if (event.data.keyLabel.toLowerCase().contains('w'))
    { keyUpPressed = (event is RawKeyDownEvent); }
  if (event.data.keyLabel.toLowerCase().contains('s'))
    { keyDownPressed = (event is RawKeyDownEvent); }
  if (event.data.keyLabel.toLowerCase().contains('r'))
    { keyRunningPressed = (event is RawKeyDownEvent); }
```

```
    return true;
  }
```

Here, we check whether the key event data key label equals the letter we mapped, and then set the appropriate variable if the key is pressed.

Note that we convert the data to lowercase in case the player has the caps lock pressed on the keyboard, which would generate a key event of S and not s.

7. Add the following import to resolve the key classes:

```
Import 'package:flutter/services.dart';
```

8. At the top of the update function and below our call to super.update(dt);, let's change the speed value based on whether the run button is pressed or whether the r key is pressed. Also, we will create a Boolean to track whether we are moving using the keys if any of our variables from *step 5* are set to true:

```
speed = (hud.runButton.buttonPressed ||
  keyRunningPressed) ? runningSpeed : walkingSpeed;
final bool isMovingByKeys = keyLeftPressed ||
  keyRightPressed || keyUpPressed || keyDownPressed;
```

9. Below this, in the update function, we have a check – if the joystick is non-zero, meaning that it is being used. This check looks like this:

```
if (!hud.joystick.delta.isZero()) {
```

Let's add an else if clause at the end of that if block for our key movement and add the following code, which will go between the if block and the else block:

```
} else if (isMovingByKeys) {
  movePlayer(dt);
  playing = true;
  movingToTouchedLocation = false;

  if (!isMoving) {
    isMoving = true;
    audioPlayerRunning = await
      FlameAudio.loopLongAudio('sounds/running.wav',
        volume: 1.0);
  }
```

```
    if (keyUpPressed && (keyLeftPressed ||
      keyRightPressed)) {
      animation = upAnimation;
      currentDirection = Character.up;
    } else if (keyDownPressed && (keyLeftPressed ||
      keyRightPressed)) {
      animation = downAnimation;
      currentDirection = Character.down;
    } else if (keyLeftPressed) {
      animation = leftAnimation;
      currentDirection = Character.left;
    } else if (keyRightPressed) {
      animation = rightAnimation;
      currentDirection = Character.right;
    } else if (keyUpPressed) {
      animation = upAnimation;
      currentDirection = Character.up;
    } else if (keyDownPressed) {
      animation = downAnimation;
      currentDirection = Character.down;
    } else {
      animation = null;
    }
```

This code works the same as the way the joystick handles movement, by trying to move our player if it doesn't collide with the water and playing the walking steps sound.

Then it sets the `animation` and `currentDirection` variables correctly based on the key pressed.

10. In the `stopAnimations` function, let's reset the movement keys when animations are stopped:

```
void stopAnimations() {
  animation?.currentIndex = 0;
  playing = false;
```

```
        keyLeftPressed = false;
        keyRightPressed = false;
        keyUpPressed = false;
        keyDownPressed = false;
    }
```

If you run the game now on the Chrome device, you will be able to control George with the keys on the keyboard.

Summary

In this chapter, we converted the game to work on the web by fixing user interface issues when resizing the browser window and allowing movement to be controlled via the keyboard.

In the next few chapters, we are going to start tackling the more advanced topics of game development, starting in the next chapter with implementing advanced graphical effects.

We will use particle effects to make our enemies explode when we kill them and use layers to create cool shadow effects for our sprites.

Questions

1. Why doesn't music play in the background when a web page first loads?

2. Why does resizing the game window cause our graphics to be drawn incorrectly?

3. Why do we have to wrap `TiledComponent` in another class to fix the user interface issues with it?

4. Which web renderers are available for building a web release?

5. What mixin do we need to use to listen for keyboard events?

Part 3: Advanced Games Programming

This part is about advanced games programming techniques to give your game extra polish and realism.

We will discuss advanced graphical effects to make your game stand out, along with building different screens for your game. We also discuss how to make your enemies appear to be intelligent by chasing the player and navigating around obstacles.

This part contains the following chapters:

- *Chapter 9, Implementing Advanced Graphics Effects*
- *Chapter 10, Making Intelligent Enemies with AI*
- *Chapter 11, Finishing the Game*

9

Implementing Advanced Graphics Effects

So far in the book, we have used graphics for animating sprite components and drawing tile maps, but there is a lot more that we can do to improve the visual aspect of the game.

In this chapter, we are going to discuss how to use particles and shadows to improve our game. We will use particle effects to make the coins and enemies explode when they are collided with and we will use layers to add a shadow effect to our sprites. These are simple yet efficient ways to improve our game visuals that run very quickly and don't affect the frame rate too much, so they are worth using to improve our game.

We will cover the following topics in this chapter:

- What are particle effects?
- Animating with particles
- Creating shadows with layers

Technical requirements

To examine the source from this chapter, you can download it from `https://github.com/PacktPublishing/Building-Games-with-Flutter/tree/main/chapter09`.

What are particle effects?

Particle effects are an easy way to create dynamic effects such as fire, smoke, explosions, and magical effects for our games. Particles have various properties that can be changed, which include the following:

- How long a particle lives

- How often a new particle is created

- The position where the particle is created

- The angle, distance, and speed of travel

- What colors the particles should be

- How physics affects the particles

A good example of a particle effect is fireworks. Fireworks explode in a variety of colors and travel at different speeds and angles as they vanish into nothing in the sky after a short time.

Flame supports many types of particle effects, which you can see examples of at `https://examples.flame-engine.org/#/Rendering_Particles`. These are discussed in more detail in the Flame documentation at `https://docs.flame-engine.org/1.0.0/particles.html`, but let's summarize some of the different types of particles here for your reference:

- `MovingParticle` – Moves the child particle between two points during its lifetime

- `AcceleratedParticle` – Applies basic physics-based effects to the particle, such as gravity or speed dampening

- `CircleParticle` – Draws circles in different sizes

- `SpriteParticle` – Uses sprite images in your particle

- `ComputedParticle` – For more advanced control of the particle, which may need computed values to affect the particle

In our game, we want to make the coins explode outward while fading out the alpha value. We will make these particles yellow to match the coin color. For our enemies, we will reuse the exploding effect but instead make the particles red to look like blood.

We will use `ComputedParticle` from the previous list of different types of particles, as we want to split the exploding particles into 12 pieces. Each of these pieces will be moving outward from the center at increasing 30-degree angles, which we will calculate with basic trigonometry. The particle will be generated and calculated from these values, and the opacity will be adjusted as it fades out based on the particle's progress.

Remember, particles have a lifespan that we can set. So, we will fade out the particle when it gets nearer to the end of its lifespan.

The actual drawing will be a simple circle with the position, angle, and opacity calculated.

Let's get started with the code for the particles in the next section.

Animating with particles

In this section, we will show you how to create great particle effects and animate them. First, we will create a new file for storing our effects in the `utils` folder, which we can use from anywhere:

1. In the `utils` folder, create a new file called `effects.dart` and open the file.

2. Add the following code for creating the exploding particle:

```
Particle explodingParticle(Vector2 origin,
  MaterialColor color) {
  double distanceToMove = 15.0;

  return Particle.generate(
    lifespan: 0.8,
    count: 12,
    generator: (i) {
      double angle = i * 30;
      double xx =
        origin.x  + (distanceToMove * cos(angle));
      double yy =
        origin.x  + (distanceToMove * sin(angle));
      Vector2 destination = Vector2(xx, yy);
```

```
        return ComputedParticle(renderer: (Canvas
          canvas, Particle particle) {
          Paint paint = Paint()..color =
            color.withOpacity(1.0 - particle.progress);
          canvas.drawCircle(Offset.zero, 1.5, paint);
        }).moving(from: origin, to: destination);
      }
    );
  }
```

Here, we have the `explodingParticle` function, which returns `ComputedParticle`. The function takes an origin position for where the particle effect should start along with a color that we should use for the particle.

We want the particle to move a short distance of `15.0`, which we use to calculate its destination position based on the angle of travel from the origin. The final destination where the particle will travel to over its lifespan is calculated using trigonometry.

We generate 12 particles at 30-degree angles, which is `12 * 30 = 360` degrees, to cover all directions outward. The lifespan is set to just under a second at `0.8`, so the explosion happens rapidly and fades away.

Finally, this is wrapped with `MovingParticle`, which moves the particle between the origin and the destination over its lifespan.

After the `lifespan` time has expired, the particle is removed from the game, so we don't need to manually monitor this as Flame does this for us by removing expiring particles from the game.

3. At the top of the `effects.dart` file, add the following imports for the particle effects:

    ```
    import 'package:flame/game.dart';
    import 'package:flame/particles.dart';
    import 'package:flutter/material.dart';
    import 'dart:math';
    ```

Let's continue by creating the particle effects in the `George` class when our player collides with a coin or an enemy.

4. Open the `george.dart` file and add the following imports:

```
import 'package:goldrush/utils/effects.dart';
import 'package:goldrush/main.dart';
import 'package:flutter/material.dart';
```

5. In the `George` class definition, we need to get a reference to the `GoldRush` class. This is needed so that when we create the particle, we base the origin position based on the world coordinates. So, let's update that code:

```
class George extends Character with KeyboardHandler,
HasGameRef<GoldRush> {
```

6. In the `onCollision` function, let's add the particle to the game via the `gameRef` reference we just added in the previous code block, where we check whether the collision is with `Zombie` or `Skeleton`:

```
if (other is Zombie || other is Skeleton) {
gameRef.add(ParticleComponent(explodingParticle(other.
position, Colors.red)));
```

7. Next, let's do the same where we check whether we have collided with a `Coin` object:

```
if (other is Coin) {
gameRef.add(ParticleComponent(explodingParticle(other.
position, Colors.yellow)));
```

If you run the game now, you will see the coins explode into yellow particles when we collide with them, and the enemies explode into red particles when we collide with them.

Now that we have some nice-looking particle effects in the game, let's move on to adding some shadows using layers in the next section.

Creating shadows with layers

Layers are a feature of Flame that allow us to group things we want to draw together or draw a prerendered graphic that doesn't change much. In your game, you may have a background that you draw once from a combination of sprites or images, but then it is used as a static image that you use as a background and draw the other moving sprites on top.

It would be inefficient to keep creating this background if it isn't changing. So, you can create it once and store it as a layer, which you can draw before you render the other game graphics.

In Flame, there are two types of layers:

- `PreRenderedLayer` – For static images
- `DynamicLayer` – For things that are moving

`PreRenderedLayer` would be suitable for backgrounds due to its static nature.

You may also want to change something in the layer and regenerate the layer, and then cache the resulting image in the layer. For example, you may want to create a weather effect in the game where the raindrops are updated and redrawn on the layer, and then this layer is drawn on top of your game world to give the impression it is raining or snowing. For this type of effect, `DynamicLayer` would be more suitable.

Flame also provides something called layer processors, which allow us to add effects to the entire layer. Currently, the only supported layer processor is called `ShadowProcessor`, which applies a shadow to the entire layer. It is possible to make your own processors though by extending the `LayerProcessor` class if you want to create other processors.

We can use `ShadowProcessor` in combination with our sprites to create a shadow behind each sprite to make them really stand out in the game. This is done by drawing our sprites into a layer after applying the shadow processor.

Let's get started by creating our layer class:

1. Open the `effects.dart` file and below the `explodingParticle` function we added earlier in *Step 2* of the *Animating with particles* section, add the following class definition for our layer:

```
class ShadowLayer extends DynamicLayer {
  final Function renderFunction;

  ShadowLayer(this.renderFunction) {
    preProcessors.add(ShadowProcessor(color:
      Colors.black, offset: const Offset(4, 4)));
  }

  @override
  void drawLayer() {
```

```
      renderFunction(canvas);
    }
  }
```

Here, we create a class called ShadowLayer, which is a DynamicLayer. In the constructor, we add the shadow processor to the list of preprocessors so that the shadow effect gets applied before drawing the sprites. Note that this is a list of preprocessors, so if you do create your own, you can add multiple effects to your layers. Also, there is a postprocessors list available too, which adds effects after your sprites are drawn if you need it.

We set the shadow to be black and drawn at an offset 4, 4 pixels away from where the sprite is drawn to give the effect of a shadow behind the sprite.

In the constructor, we pass a function reference that is then used when we call drawLayer(). We do this because we want to hold a reference to the super class render function, so that we delegate the drawing to the layer. So, our sprites will draw onto the layer where they will have their shadow applied, and then we call on the super class to draw the layer to the game, based on whatever animation frame we are currently rendering.

Because of this, when we render our sprites in the render function, we will render into ShadowLayer and not make a call to the super class there, or we will be drawing twice, which is inefficient and not needed.

2. Now, at the top of the file, let's add an import for the layer package:

    ```
    import 'package:flame/layers.dart';
    ```

    Next, let's set up the Coin class first and add a shadow to all our coins, so we can see how this delegated rendering works in practice.

3. Open the coin.dart file and add the following import at the top of the file:

    ```
    import 'package:goldrush/utils/effects.dart';
    ```

4. In the Coin class, add a variable to store ShadowLayer below where we store originalPosition:

    ```
    late Vector2 originalPosition;
    late ShadowLayer shadowLayer;
    ```

5. Add the following import for `ShadowLayer`:

    ```
    import 'package:goldrush/utils/effects.dart';
    ```

6. At the bottom of the `onLoad` function, add the following line to initialize the shadow layer:

    ```
    shadowLayer = ShadowLayer(super.render);
    ```

    Here, we can see we are passing the function reference to the super class render function.

7. At the bottom of the `Coin` class, add the following override for the render function, which delegates the drawing to `shadowLayer`:

    ```
    @override
    void render(Canvas canvas) {
      shadowLayer.render(canvas);
    }
    ```

    If you run the game now, you will see our shadow effect behind all the coins in the game.

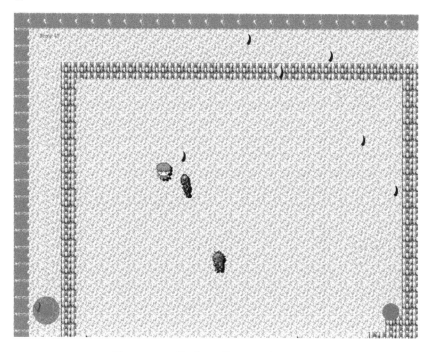

Figure 9.1 – Shadow effects on the sprites

Let's continue and apply the same effect to our enemy sprites and our player sprite, George.

We will add this to the `Character` class, which is the base class for George and our enemies, to reduce duplicate code.

8. Open the `character.dart` file and add the following import for the layer package:

    ```
    import 'package:goldrush/utils/effects.dart';
    ```

9. In the `Character` class, add a variable to store `ShadowLayer` below where we store `originalPosition`:

    ```
    late Vector2 originalPosition;
    late ShadowLayer shadowLayer;
    ```

10. Add the following `onLoad` function to the `Character` class to initialize the shadow layer:

    ```
    @override
    Future<void> onLoad() async {
      super.onLoad();

      shadowLayer = ShadowLayer(super.render);
    }
    ```

11. Finally, add the `render` function to the `Character` class to delegate the drawing to `shadowLayer`:

    ```
    @override
    void render(Canvas canvas) {
      shadowLayer.render(canvas);
    }
    ```

    Note that you may see a message about calling the `render` function of the super class, but we want to avoid this as it will be called from within our shadow layer, so it is omitted here.

If you run the game now, you will see that our player and enemies now have lovely shadow effects behind them, which really makes them stand out nicely against the background!

Summary

In this chapter, we learned how to apply advanced graphical effects to our game to make the game look much better. We added particle effects to make the coins and enemies explode when collided with and added some nice shadow effects behind our player, enemies, and coins.

In the next chapter, we are going to discuss how to make our player and enemies appear more intelligent by adding game **Artificial Intelligence** (**AI**) to them.

We will change the behavior of the enemies – instead of us attacking them, they will attack us! The enemies will chase George when he gets too near to them and will still explode when they hit us, but we will add a health value to George that will decrease if we collide with an exploding enemy. Also, the enemies will only chase if they are facing and can see George and are within a certain distance.

Plus, we will add some further obstacles to our game and show you how to use pathfinding to make sure George walks around obstacles in our game world when moving, by touching the screen.

Questions

1. What are some properties that are common to particle effects?

2. Why do particles need to be removed from the game by setting a lifespan?

3. What are some examples of particles that Flame supports?

4. What are the different types of layers that Flame supports?

5. Why do we need to delegate the rendering of the super class to the layer class?

10
Making Intelligent Enemies with AI

The game is coming along nicely now, but there isn't really any challenge to it yet. We collect the coins or kill our enemies, but that's all very predictable and easy.

In this chapter, we are going to change the game to make it more challenging by adding a health value to our player, George, and making the enemies chase us instead, reducing our health for each enemy that hits us. If our health gets to zero, we lose the game. So, the objective will be to collect the coins while avoiding the enemies.

To make the enemies appear more intelligent, we will use very simple **Artificial Intelligence (AI)** algorithms for the enemies to detect when George is nearby and, when they can see him, their movement will change from random movements to moving in George's direction to attack him.

We will then add some extra water to the map as obstacles and discuss how to move from your origin to the destination while avoiding the water and walking around it to reach your destination.

We will cover the following topics in this chapter:

- Making enemies chase the player
- Navigating obstacles with pathfinding

Technical requirements

To examine the source from this chapter, you can download it from `https://github.com/PacktPublishing/Building-Games-with-Flutter/tree/main/chapter10`.

The following steps will add a library to the `pubspec` file to assist with pathfinding, along with some new and updated assets:

1. In this chapter, we will use updated versions of the tile map files, so please download these updated tile map files and place them in the `assets/tiles` folder, overriding the existing files:

    `https://github.com/PacktPublishing/Building-Games-with-Flutter/blob/main/chapter10/assets/tiles/tiles.tmx`

    `https://github.com/PacktPublishing/Building-Games-with-Flutter/blob/main/chapter10/assets/tiles/tiles.tsx`

2. Open the `pubspec.yaml` file and add the following dependency:

    ```
    a_star_algorithm: ^0.3.0
    ```

3. In this chapter, we will use a modified version of the sprite sheet for our character George, so let's update that.

    Download the `george.png` image from the following URL, `https://raw.githubusercontent.com/PacktPublishing/Building-Games-with-Flutter/main/chapter10/assets/images/george.png`, and overwrite the file in the `assets/images` folder. Note that as we already have a reference in the `pubspec.yaml` file for `george.png`, we don't need to do anything further with it.

4. Save the file and allow `pub get` to download this dependency and validate the assets:

    ```
    flutter pub get
    ```

Making enemies chase the player

There are two main challenges associated with making enemies chase the player that we need to overcome, making the player believe the enemy is showing intelligence and is hunting them down. They are as follows:

- The first is that the player is near enough to the enemy so that the enemy may see or hear them. You don't want enemies to start chasing players when they are on the other side of the map, otherwise, the effect is lost and isn't believable.

- The second is that the enemy is facing the player when they start chasing. If the enemy is walking in the opposite direction, the player might be able to sneak past them without the enemy noticing. So we won't make them chase when they are not even facing the player.

To overcome these challenges, we will track the distance between the player and enemy at every update, which happens 60 times per second. If the distance between them is below a certain value, and if the angle between the player and enemy indicates that the enemy is facing the player, then we will start the enemy chasing the player. If the player can run away from the enemy, then the enemy will return to its normal movement pattern. We will also change the enemies' speed so that the normal movement speed is trebled when they are chasing.

Let's get started by making the enemies chase the player:

1. Open the `character_enemy.dart` file and, outside of the class definition, add the following enum for defining whether we are walking about or chasing the player:

   ```
   enum EnemyMovementType {
     WALKING,
     CHASING
   }
   ```

2. In the `EnemyCharacter` class, below the constructor, add the following variables:

   ```
   Character playerToTrack;
   EnemyMovementType enemyMovementType =
     EnemyMovementType.WALKING;
   static const DISTANCE _ TO _ TRACK = 150.0;
   double walkingSpeed, chasingSpeed;
   ```

Here, we create variables for tracking the character we want to chase and set the enemy movement type to walking by default. We set a constant for the distance check that we will use for detecting whether the enemy is near to the player and create some values for maintaining the walking and chasing speeds.

3. Change the constructor to the following code to set up some of the values we created in *step 2*:

```
EnemyCharacter({required Character player, required
  Vector2 position, required Vector2 size, required
    double speed}) :
  playerToTrack = player,
  walkingSpeed = speed,
  chasingSpeed = speed * 2,
  super(position: position, size: size, speed: speed);
```

Here, we set up the chasing speed to be twice as fast as our walking speed.

4. Let's import the math_utils.dart file so that we can use the getAngle function to determine whether this enemy is facing the player:

```
import 'package:goldrush/utils/math _ utils.dart';
```

5. Next, let's create a function called isPlayerNearAndVisible to check that the player is close by and visible to the enemy by facing in the player's direction:

```
bool isPlayerNearAndVisible() {
  bool isPlayerNear = position.distanceTo(
    playerToTrack.position) < DISTANCE _ TO _ TRACK;
  bool isEnemyFacingPlayer = false;
  var angle =
    getAngle(position, playerToTrack.position);
  if ((angle > 315 && angle < 360) || (angle > 0 &&
    angle < 45) ) { // Facing right
    isEnemyFacingPlayer = currentDirection ==
      Character.right;
  } else if (angle > 45 && angle < 135) {
    // Facing down
    isEnemyFacingPlayer = currentDirection ==
      Character.down;
```

```
    } else if (angle > 135 && angle < 225) {
      // Facing left
      isEnemyFacingPlayer = currentDirection ==
        Character.left;
    } else if (angle > 225 && angle < 315) {
      // Facing up
      isEnemyFacingPlayer = currentDirection ==
        Character.up;
    }
    return isPlayerNear && isEnemyFacingPlayer;
  }
```

In the `isPlayerNearAndVisible` function, we first measure the distance to the player from our enemy position, check whether it is less than our `DISTANCE_TO_TRACK` value, and then set the `isPlayerNear` value to `true` if needed.

Next, we use the `getAngle` function to get the angle between the enemy and player and then use this to check whether the angle we are facing matches the `currentDirection` we are facing. If this matches, then the enemy is facing the player and we set the `isEnemyFacingPlayer` flag as needed.

If both values are `true`, we will return `true` from this function to indicate the enemy is near enough and can see the player, which we will use in the `update` function next to change the `enemyMovementType` from walking to chasing.

6. Let's rewrite the `update` function in the `EnemyCharacter` class. First, remove the existing `update` function and replace it with the code from GitHub at `https://github.com/PacktPublishing/Building-Games-with-Flutter/blob/main/chapter10/lib/components/character_enemy.dart`.

Let's go through the changes we have made to this function.

The previous `update` code is now in a `switch/case` block if the enemy is in the default walking state. We initially call the `isPlayerNearAndVisible` function we created in *Step 4* and set our current speed to `chasingSpeed` if the player is near and visible, and to `walkingSpeed` if not.

If the `enemyMovementType` is `WALKING`, the enemy will walk around as before, but when `CHASING`, the enemy will run directly toward the player at the increased speed.

7. Now, let's update the `Skeleton` and `Zombie` classes to take a reference to the player class, `George`, which extends from the `Character` class, and pass this reference to the `EnemyCharacter` base class.

    Open the `skeleton.dart` file and change the constructor like this:

    ```
    Skeleton({required Character player, required Vector2
        position, required Vector2 size, required double
            speed}) : super(player: player, position:
                position, size: size, speed: speed) {
    ```

8. Open the `zombie.dart` file and change the constructor like this:

    ```
    Zombie({required Character player, required Vector2
        position, required Vector2 size, required double
            speed}) : super(player: player, position:
                position, size: size, speed: speed) {
    ```

9. Add the following import to resolve the reference to `Character` in the constructor:

    ```
    import 'package:goldrush/components/character.dart';
    ```

10. Let's now tie all this together by passing the player reference to the enemy classes.

    Open the `main.dart` file and change the code where you add the enemies like this:

    ```
    if (index % 2 == 0) {
      add(Skeleton(player: george, position:
        Vector2(position.x + gameScreenBounds.left,
          position.y + gameScreenBounds.top), size:
            Vector2(32.0, 64.0), speed: 20.0));
    } else {
      add (Zombie(player: george, position:
        Vector2(position.x + gameScreenBounds.left,
          position.y + gameScreenBounds.top), size:
            Vector2(32.0, 64.0), speed: 20.0));
    }
    ```

11. Also, because we changed the George's image earlier, we need to update the new size to 32, 32, where we create George in the onLoad function of main.dart:

```
var george = George(barrierOffsets: barrierOffsets,
   hud: hud, position: Vector2(gameScreenBounds.left +
      300, gameScreenBounds.top + 300), size:
         Vector2(32.0, 32.0), speed: 40.0);
```

If you run the game now and move George near to an enemy while the enemy is facing George, you will see the enemy chase George. If the enemy catches George, you will see the enemy collide and explode, as discussed previously in the *Animating with particles* section of *Chapter 9, Implementing Advanced Graphics Effects*.

Let's change this now to give George a health value of 100%, which we will reduce by 25% every time an enemy attacks George and not increase our score. In the next chapter, we will add some user interface screens that will show **Game Over** when George's health reaches 0, but for now, we will just get the mechanism working.

12. In the hud folder, create a new file called health_text.dart and add the code from here: https://github.com/PacktPublishing/Building-Games-with-Flutter/blob/main/chapter10/lib/components/hud/health_text.dart.

This code block will look very familiar as it's the same as the ScoreText component, but with all the references to score changed to health.

13. Open the hud.dart file and add the following import:

```
import
   'package:goldrush/components/hud/health _ text.dart';
```

14. At the top of the HudComponent class, add the following variable to show the HealthText value:

```
late HealthText healthText;
```

15. In the onGameResize function, at the bottom of the if block, change the code as follows to initialize the healthText value and add it to the HUD:

```
scoreText = ScoreText(position: Vector2(
   gameScreenBounds.left + 80, gameScreenBounds.top +
      60));
healthText = HealthText(position: Vector2(
```

```
    gameScreenBounds.right - 80, gameScreenBounds.top +
      60));
```

```
add(joystick);
add(runButton);
add(scoreText);
add(healthText);
```

16. At the bottom of the `else` block in the same function, add the following line to update the `healthText` position:

```
joystick.position = Vector2(gameScreenBounds.left +
    80, gameScreenBounds.bottom - 80);
RunButton.position = Vector2(gameScreenBounds.right -
    80, gameScreenBounds.bottom - 80);
scoreText.position = Vector2(gameScreenBounds.left +
    80, gameScreenBounds.top + 60);
healthText.position = Vector2(gameScreenBounds.right -
    80, gameScreenBounds.top + 60);
```

17. Open the `george.dart` file and, in the variables section at the top, add the following code:

```
int health = 100;
```

18. In the `onCollision` function, let's change the `if` block to check whether we have hit a `Zombie` or `Skeleton`, so the code looks like the following:

```
if (other is Zombie || other is Skeleton) {
  gameRef.add(ParticleComponent(explodingParticle(
    other.position, Colors.red)));
  other.removeFromParent();
  if (health > 0) {
    health -= 25;
    hud.healthText.setHealth(health);
  } else {
    // TODO: Show game over screen here
  }
```

```
FlameAudio.play('sounds/enemy _ dies.wav', volume:
   1.0);
}
```

If you run the code now, you will see the health value in the top-right corner, which will reduce every time you collide with an enemy, as shown in the following figure:

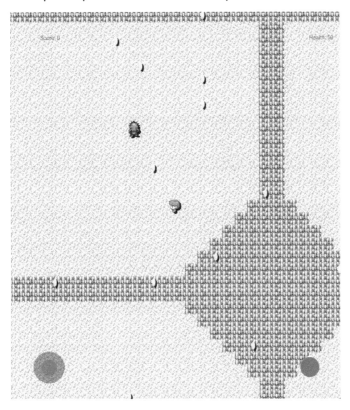

Figure 10.1 – Health score reduced when hit by an enemy

In the next section, we will add some water obstacles to the map and discuss how to navigate around them. We will also discuss how we can enhance our enemies' AI, meaning that they will not chase you if they can't see you because they are blocked by a water obstacle.

Navigating obstacles with pathfinding

In this section, we will discuss how to move our character from A to B when there are obstacles in the way. There are many solutions to this problem, but a common solution in games development that we are going to use is called the **A Star algorithm**.

The algorithm is an efficient way to calculate a route on a 2D grid. Remember, a tile map is a 2D grid that uses tile IDs to represent what is drawn on the map. We provide the algorithm with our grid coordinates for our start location (the current location of George) and our end location (where we tap on the screen), along with a list of grid coordinates for any obstacles that are in the way. The algorithm then returns a list of grid offsets that represent a path, which we can follow to navigate to our touched location while avoiding all obstacles!

Our initial challenge is that when we move George around, we are using pixels to represent the location, but the algorithm works in grid coordinates. For instance, if George was at the top left of the map (ignoring the water), his pixel coordinate might be 48, 48, but his grid coordinate will be 1, 1.

Let's start by creating a new file with some helper functions that let us convert between George's world coordinate (pixel) and his grid coordinate:

1. First, create and open a new file in the utils folder called map_utils.dart, and then add the following code:

    ```
    import 'package:flame/components.dart';
    import 'package:flutter/material.dart';

    const  int TILE _ SIZE = 32;

    Offset worldToGridOffset(Vector2 mapLocation) {
      double x =
        (mapLocation.x / TILE _ SIZE).floor().toDouble();
      double y =
        (mapLocation.y / TILE _ SIZE).floor().toDouble();

      return Offset(x, y);
    }

    Vector2 gridOffsetToWorld(Offset gridOffset) {
      double x = (gridOffset.dx * TILE _ SIZE);
      double y = (gridOffset.dy * TILE _ SIZE);

      return Vector2(x, y);
    }
    ```

Here, we have two functions for converting between the world and grid coordinates while taking into account our tile size of 32 x 32.

Next, we will update our George class to update our code when we move to a touched location, to first calculate the path with the A Star algorithm, and then navigate along the path while changing the direction we are facing as we navigate the path.

2. Open the george.dart file and add the following imports to the file:

```dart
import 'package:goldrush/utils/map_utils.dart';
import
  'package:a_star_algorithm/a_star_algorithm.dart';
```

3. Next, add the following variables at the top of the class to keep track of the barrier offset locations, our path to the destination, and our current path step:

```dart
List<Offset> barrierOffsets;
List<Offset> pathToTargetLocation = [];
int currentPathStep = -1;
```

4. Let's now update the constructor to pass in the barrierOffsets:

```dart
George({required this.barrierOffsets, required
    this.hud, required Vector2 position, required
      Vector2 size, required double speed}) : super(
        position: position, size: size, speed: speed) {
```

5. Next, let's update the moveToLocation function to set up the new variables:

```dart
void moveToLocation(TapUpInfo info) {
  pathToTargetLocation = AStar(
    rows: 50,
    columns: 50,
    start: worldToGridOffset(position),
    end: worldToGridOffset(info.eventPosition.game),
    withDiagonal: true,
    barriers: barrierOffsets
  ).findThePath().toList();
  targetLocation = info.eventPosition.game;
  faceCorrectDirection();
```

As `pathToTargetLocation[0]` is the same as the current position, we set `currentPathStep` to the next step, 1:

```
currentPathStep = 1;
targetLocation = gridOffsetToWorld(
    pathToTargetLocation[currentPathStep]);
targetLocation.add(Vector2(16, 16));
movingToTouchedLocation = true;
}
```

Here, we store the result of the A Star algorithm in the `pathToTargetLocation` variable.

We pass in our number of rows and columns, which is the same as our map size, `50 x 50`. We set the `withDiagonal` value to allow the path to take shortcuts, which looks more natural. You can try setting this value to `false` when we run this code to see the difference and to decide your preference. We pass in `barrierOffsets`, which will be passed in via the constructor. Finally, we convert George's position and the touched location to the grid offset coordinates. The result will be a path to the location while avoiding the water obstacles.

If you load the updated map that we downloaded in the *Technical requirements* section of this chapter into the Tiled application, you will see that we have placed water obstacles in the center of the map, which we can use to test that the path navigation works.

After getting the A Star result, we set `targetLocation` to be the touched location, and then call a new function that we will define soon, called `faceCorrectDirection`. This new function ensures that George is facing the correct direction when he starts navigating the path to the target location.

Next, we set `currentPathStep` to start at `1`, rather than at the start of the list in position `0`. This is because, when we get the result of the algorithm, it inserts our current location at position `0` and, as we are already at that location, we don't need to move there!

We then set `targetLocation` based on the offset at the `currentPathStep` to 1 and convert this back to world coordinates for our movement. Remember, we need to use grid coordinates in order for the algorithm to work, but we require world coordinates for our movement in real pixels. Finally, we add a vector of `16, 16` to our `targetLocation`.

This is because, when we convert to world coordinates, we are basing this on the top-left corner of the tile, but we want to move George based on the center of the tile, so we add `16, 16` to the *x* and *y* values of the vectors, which is half of the tile size, 32.

Finally in this function, we set `movingToTouchedLocation` to `true`, which starts George moving toward the `targetLocation` in the `update` function.

6. Next, we need to change the `update` function to walk along the path. This function allows us to change the next path step by walking between each path step until we reach the final point in the path.

In the previous step, we referenced a new function called `faceCurrentDirection`, which we will also use again when we change the `update` function, so let's create that first.

Below the `update` function, create a new function called `faceCurrentDirection` and add the following code:

```
void faceCorrectDirection() {
    var angle = getAngle(position, targetLocation);
    if ((angle > 315 && angle < 360) || (angle > 0 &&
      angle < 45) ) { // Facing right
      animation = rightAnimation;
      currentDirection = Character.right;
    }
    else if (angle > 45 && angle < 135) {
      // Facing down
      animation = downAnimation;
      currentDirection = Character.down;
    }
    else if (angle > 135 && angle < 225) {
      // Facing left
      animation = leftAnimation;
      currentDirection = Character.left;
    }
    else if (angle > 225 && angle < 315) {
      // Facing up
      animation = upAnimation;
```

```
            currentDirection = Character.up;
        }
    }
```

7. Finally in this step, we are going to change the `update` function to change the `targetLocation` when each path step is taken until we reach our touched location.

    Because the `update` function is quite large now, we are going to refactor this function completely to make it easier to manage our code.

    We will create three new functions for each movement type, `moveByJoystick`, `moveByKeyboard`, and `moveByTouch`. We will move the relevant parts of the `update` function into the first two functions, but for the third, we will do a rewrite because we are now using our path around the obstacles.

    Below our `update` function, add the following three empty function stubs to start:

    ```
    void moveByJoystick(double dt) async {}
    void moveByKeyboard(double dt) async {}
    void moveByTouch(double dt) async {}
    ```

8. Next, add the code (available at `https://github.com/PacktPublishing/Building-Games-with-Flutter/blob/main/chapter10/lib/components/george.dart`) from the `update` function to the `moveByJoystick` function.

9. Next, add the following code from the `update` function to the `moveByKeyboard` function:

    ```
    movePlayer(dt);
    playing = true;
    movingToTouchedLocation = false;

    if (!isMoving) {
      isMoving = true;
      audioPlayerRunning = await FlameAudio.loopLongAudio(
        'sounds/running.wav', volume: 1.0);
    }

    if (keyUpPressed && (keyLeftPressed ||
      keyRightPressed)) {
    ```

```
    animation = upAnimation;
    currentDirection = Character.up;
  } else if (keyDownPressed && (keyLeftPressed ||
    keyRightPressed)) {
    animation = downAnimation;
    currentDirection = Character.down;
  } else if (keyLeftPressed) {
    animation = leftAnimation;
    currentDirection = Character.left;
  } else if (keyRightPressed) {
    animation = rightAnimation;
    currentDirection = Character.right;
  } else if (keyUpPressed) {
    animation = upAnimation;
    currentDirection = Character.up;
  } else if (keyDownPressed) {
    animation = downAnimation;
    currentDirection = Character.down;
  } else {
    animation = null;
  }
```

10. Next, add the following code from the `update` function to the `moveByTouch` function:

```
if (!isMoving) {
  isMoving = true;
  audioPlayerRunning = await FlameAudio.loopLongAudio(
    'sounds/running.wav', volume: 1.0);
}

movePlayer(dt);
double threshold = 2.0;
var difference = targetLocation - position;
if (difference.x.abs() < threshold &&
    difference.y.abs() < threshold) {
  if (currentPathStep < pathToTargetLocation.length -
```

```
        1) {
        currentPathStep++;
        targetLocation = gridOffsetToWorld(
          pathToTargetLocation[currentPathStep]);
        targetLocation.add(Vector2(16, 16));
      } else {
        stopAnimations();
        audioPlayerRunning.stop();
        isMoving = false;

        movingToTouchedLocation = false;
        return;
      }
    }

    playing = true;
    if (currentPathStep <= pathToTargetLocation.length) {
      faceCorrectDirection();
    }
}
```

In the moveByTouch function, we have changed a few things – so let's go through the parts that are different from our previous touch code discussed in earlier chapters.

We still check whether our location after moving the player is within the threshold, but we have increased the threshold to 2.0, which helps with touch to move, especially when the character is running. If we have arrived at the targetLocation, we check whether there are any more steps and increase currentPathStep if there are more steps, and then update targetLocation to the new path location. Once again, because each offset in the path relates to the top-left corner of the grid cell, we add 16, 16 to the target location to center it. If there are no more steps, we stop the animation and sound.

At each step change, we adjust the direction the character is facing to ensure that the character faces the direction of travel to the next path step.

11. Now that we have our three movement functions defined, let's rewrite the simplified
    `update` function. Replace the current `update` function in its entirety with the
    following new code that uses our new movement functions:

```
@override
void update(double dt) async {
  super.update(dt);

  speed = (hud.runButton.buttonPressed ||
    keyRunningPressed) ? runningSpeed : walkingSpeed;
  final bool isMovingByKeys = keyLeftPressed ||
    keyRightPressed || keyUpPressed || keyDownPressed;

  if (!hud.joystick.delta.isZero()) {
    moveByJoystick(dt);
  } else if (isMovingByKeys) {
      moveByKeyboard(dt);
  } else {
    if (movingToTouchedLocation) {
      moveByTouch(dt);
    } else {
      if (playing) {
        stopAnimations();
      }
      if (isMoving) {
        isMoving = false;
        audioPlayerRunning.stop();
      }
    }
  }
}
```

Now that we have finished updating the `George` class, let's move on to the main
class to connect everything together.

12. Open the `main.dart` file and add the following import for the map utils functions:

```
import 'package:goldrush/utils/map_utils.dart';
```

13. In the onLoad function, below where we load and play the background music, add
the following code to initialize the water barriers and then pass these to the George
class via the constructor for use with pathfinding:

```
FlameAudio.bgm.initialize();
await FlameAudio.bgm.load('music/music.mp3');
await FlameAudio.bgm.play('music/music.mp3', volume:
   0.1);

final tiledMap = await TiledComponent.load(
   'tiles.tmx', Vector2.all(32));
add(TileMapComponent(tiledMap));

List<Offset> barrierOffsets = [];
final water =
   tiledMap.tileMap.getObjectGroupFromLayer('Water');
water.objects.forEach((rect) {
   if (rect.width == 32 && rect.height == 32) {
     barrierOffsets.add(worldToGridOffset(Vector2(
       rect.x, rect.y)));
   }
   add(Water(position: Vector2(rect.x +
    gameScreenBounds.left, rect.y +
      gameScreenBounds.top), size: Vector2(rect.width,
        rect.height), id: rect.id));
});

var hud = HudComponent();
var george = George(barrierOffsets: barrierOffsets,
   hud: hud, position: Vector2(gameScreenBounds.left +
     300, gameScreenBounds.top + 300), size:
       Vector2(32.0, 32.0), speed: 40.0);
add (george);
children.changePriority(george, 15);
```

Please note that we have moved the code for initializing the tile map and water
objects, meaning you can remove the other references for that in this function.

If you run the game now and use touch to move toward the center of the map inside of the water barriers, you will see George walk around the water barriers to get to his location!

Summary

In this chapter, we improved our character and enemies by making them appear more intelligent. The enemies now chase George if he is near enough and within their line of sight, and George can now move around the map while avoiding obstacles.

In the final chapter, we will add some new screens to the game to tie everything together.

We will add a simple menu intro screen with a link to a settings screen and talk about how we can navigate between screens within the game. We will also discuss how you could improve the game further, how to monetize your games, and what else is worth learning to expand your games' programming skills.

Questions

1. What function can we call to measure the distance between two positions to detect whether an enemy is near a player?

2. What is the name of the algorithm we use for pathfinding in our game?

3. How can we convert between world and grid coordinates?

4. Why would we set `withDiagonal` to `true` in our pathfinding algorithm?

5. Why must we adjust the direction in which we are facing at each step of our pathfinding?

11
Finishing the Game

The game is looking great and is nearly complete, but we want to tie up some loose ends in this chapter to finish it off. At the moment, we only have the main game screen; however, games often have many screens in them, such as a menu screen or settings screen.

In this chapter, we will add a few more screens and show you how to navigate between them. We will create these screens with standard Flutter widgets and show you how you can mix Flutter and Flame together. Specifically, in our settings screen, we will add an option for controlling the music volume and persist the user's music volume preference, and then use this when playing the game.

After wrapping up the game code, we will discuss a few other things to consider when developing a game, such as how to make money from it, what else is worth learning as you continue to learn more about game development, and where to get help when you get stuck developing your games.

We will cover the following topics in this chapter:

- Wrapping up the game
- Monetizing your game
- What else should I learn?
- Where to get help?

Technical requirements

To examine the source from this chapter, you can download it from `https://github.com/PacktPublishing/Building-Games-with-Flutter/tree/main/chapter11`.

In this chapter, we will save the user's preference for the music volume, so let's add the library for persisting this value in our game:

1. Open the `pubspec.yaml` file and add the following dependency:

    ```
    shared _ preferences: ^2.0.15
    ```

2. Save the file and allow `pub get` to download this dependency and validate the assets:

    ```
    flutter pub get
    ```

In the next section, we will discuss the final code we need to add to the game to wrap things up, including the game screens and navigation.

Wrapping up the game

In this section, we will add three new screens and navigate between these screens.

These screens are as follows:

*   **Menu screen**: The first screen the player will see, with options to play the game, view the settings, or exit the game.

*   **Settings screen**: The settings allow us to change the music volume via a `Slider` widget or go back to the menu screen.

*   **Game over screen**: We will show this screen when the player's health is 0 and allow them to go back to the menu screen to play again.

These three screens will use standard Flutter widgets; we will use Flutter navigation routes to navigate between them and our game widget to play the game.

Let's get started by adding each of these screens.

Adding a menu screen

In this section, we will add a menu screen to help us navigate between each of the game's screens by following these steps:

1. In the project's `lib` directory, create a new folder called `widgets` to hold our new widget screens.

2. Create three new files in the `widgets` folder called `screen_menu.dart`, `screen_settings.dart`, and `screen_gameover.dart`.

3. Open the `screen_menu.dart` file and add the following code:

    ```dart
    import 'package:flutter/material.dart';
    import 'package:flutter/services.dart';

    class MenuScreen extends StatelessWidget {
      const MenuScreen({Key? key}) : super(key: key);

      @override
      Widget build(BuildContext context) {
        return Scaffold(
          backgroundColor: Colors.black,
          body: Center(
            child: Column(
              mainAxisAlignment: MainAxisAlignment.center,
              crossAxisAlignment:
                CrossAxisAlignment.center,
              children: [
                getGameTitle(),
                getGameMenu(context)
              ]
            )
          ),
        );
      }
    ```

```
Widget getGameTitle() {}

Widget getGameMenu(BuildContext context) {}
}
```

Here, we add a class called `MenuScreen`, which is `StatelessWidget`, and set up the basic structure for the layout, where we will have a title at the top and a few menu items that we can click on in the menu.

4. Let's expand the `getGameTitle` function to return a `Text` widget for the title:

```
Widget getGameTitle() {
  return Text('Gold Rush', style: TextStyle(color:
    Colors.yellow, fontSize: 64.0));
}
```

5. Next, we will expand the `getGameMenu` function to add menu options for **Play Game**, **Settings**, and **Exit Game**; they will be `Text` widgets wrapped in `GestureDetector` widgets so that they are clickable.

For the first two options, we will use navigator routes to move to the new screens, and we will use a `SystemNavigator` function to exit the game:

```
Widget getGameMenu(BuildContext context) {
  return Padding(
    padding: const EdgeInsets.all(40.0),
    child: Column(children: [
      Padding(
        padding: const EdgeInsets.all(8.0),
        child: GestureDetector(
          onTap: () {
            Navigator.pushNamedAndRemoveUntil(context,
              "/game", (r) => false);
          },
          child: Text('Play Game', style: TextStyle(
            color: Colors.blue, fontSize: 32.0))),
        ),
      Padding(
        padding: const EdgeInsets.all(8.0),
        child: GestureDetector(
```

```
        onTap: () {
          Navigator.pushNamedAndRemoveUntil(context,
            "/settings", (r) => false);
        },
        child: Text('Settings', style: TextStyle(
          color: Colors.blue, fontSize: 32.0))),
      ),
      Padding(
        padding: const EdgeInsets.all(8.0),
        child: GestureDetector(
          onTap: () { SystemNavigator.pop(); },
        child: Text('Exit Game', style: TextStyle(
          color: Colors.red, fontSize: 32.0))),
        ),
    ]),
  );
}
```

Here, we have a simple widget that draws the menu, which is a simple column of menu items in the middle, with a title at the top and an exit option below the menu items. Clicking on these options tells the navigator to change to a different page.

Here, you can see how the menu screen should look:

Figure 11.1 – The game menu screen, allowing you to play the game or view the settings

Next, let's continue for now with the settings screen.

Adding a settings screen

In this section, we will add a settings screen to allow us to choose the volume of the background music by following these steps:

1. Open the `screen_settings.dart` file and add the code from here: `https://github.com/PacktPublishing/Building-Games-with-Flutter/blob/main/chapter11/lib/widgets/screen_settings.dart`.

    In this code block, we will set up `StatefulWidget` this time, as we want to keep track of the music volume value and persist this for using the `SharedPreferences` library we added earlier in the *Technical requirements* section.

    We store the current music volume in a variable called `musicVolume`. In the `initState` function, we try and read this value from the shared preferences and set it to `25%` as a default if this has not been previously set.

    Let's continue and build the UI for the settings screen by completing the empty functions.

2. Here is the code for the `getSettingsTitle` function:

    ```
    Widget getSettingsTitle() {
      return Padding(
        padding: const EdgeInsets.fromLTRB(0, 0, 0, 20),
        child: Text('Settings', style: TextStyle(color:
          Colors.yellow, fontSize: 64.0)),
      );
    }
    ```

    Here, we return a `Text` widget for our title, which is styled in yellow and has a font size of `64`.

3. The following is the code for the `getMusicVolumeLabel` function:

    ```
    Widget getMusicVolumeLabel() {
      return Text('Music Volume', style: TextStyle(color:
        Colors.blue, fontSize: 32.0));
    }
    ```

    Here, we return a `Text` widget for our volume label, which is styled in blue and has a font size of `32`.

The following is the code for the `getVolumeSlider` function:

```
Widget getVolumeSlider() {
  return SizedBox(
    width: 250.0,
    child: Slider(
      value: musicVolume,
      min: 0.0,
      max: 100.0,
      label: '${musicVolume.round()}',
      divisions: 4,
      onChanged: (double newMusicVolume) {
        SharedPreferences.getInstance().then((prefs)
          => prefs.setDouble('musicVolume',
            newMusicVolume));
        setState(() => musicVolume = newMusicVolume);
      }),
  );
}
```

Here, we return a `Slider` widget wrapped around a fixed `SizedBox` widget that has values for the music volume between `0` and `100`. Whenever the slider value is changed, we set the `musicVolume` value in the widget and save this to the shared preferences.

4. The following is the code for the `getBackLabel` function:

```
Widget getBackLabel() {
  return GestureDetector(
    onTap: () { Navigator.pushNamedAndRemoveUntil(
      context, "/", (r) => false); },
    child: Text('Back', style: TextStyle(color:
      Colors.red, fontSize: 32.0))
  );}
```

Here, we return a `Text` label to go back to the main menu and use `Navigator` to return the player to the top-level route if this is clicked.

The following screenshot shows our settings screen along with a slider to set the music volume:

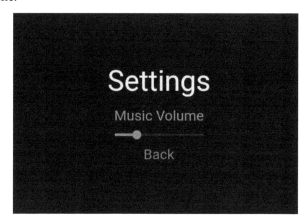

Figure 11.2 – The Settings screen with the adjustable music volume

Now that the settings screen is complete, let's work on our final screen, which is the game over screen.

Adding a game over screen

In this section, we will add a game over screen to let the user know the game has ended. To do this, open the `screen_gameover.dart` file and add the code from here: `https://github.com/PacktPublishing/Building-Games-with-Flutter/blob/main/chapter11/lib/widgets/screen_gameover.dart`.

In this code block, we show a simple screen to indicate that the game is over and a link to go back to the menu, where the user can play again, change the settings, or quit the game.

Here is the game over screen that is shown when George dies:

Figure 11.3 – The game over screen when George dies

Now that we have our three extra screens, let's tie these together with navigation routes and music volume.

Compiling all screens with navigation routes and music volume

In this section, we will tie all the navigation together and also adjust the music volume, based on the settings menu choice. To do this, we will follow these steps:

1. Open the `main.dart` file and import the screens and shared preference library:

    ```
    import
      'package:goldrush/widgets/screen_gameover.dart';
    import 'package:goldrush/widgets/screen_menu.dart';
    import
      'package:goldrush/widgets/screen_settings.dart';
    import
      'package:shared_preferences/shared_preferences.dart';
    ```

2. Let's rewrite the `main` function to use routes. Replace the existing `main` function with the following:

    ```
    void main() async {
      WidgetsFlutterBinding.ensureInitialized();
      await Flame.device.fullScreen();
      await Flame.device.setLandscape();

      runApp(
        MaterialApp(
          debugShowCheckedModeBanner: false,
          title: 'Gold Rush',
          initialRoute: '/',
          routes: {
            '/': (context) => MenuScreen(),
            '/settings': (context) => SettingsScreen(),
            '/gameover': (context) => GameOverScreen(),
            '/game': (context) => GameWidget(game:
              GoldRush()),
    ```

```
      },
    ),
  );
}
```

Here, we set the screen up as full-screen landscape as we did before in *Chapter 7, Designing Your Own Levels*, but now we have four navigation routes defaulting, with the initial route pointing to the menu screen.

3. In the onLoad function of the GoldRush class, let's read the musicVolume value from shared preferences and set up the playback of the music with this value. Note that if the player has not gone into the settings and changed this value, the volume will default to 25%.

   Returning to where the background audio is initialized, add the following code:

   ```
   var musicVolume;
   await SharedPreferences.getInstance()
     .then((prefs) => prefs.getDouble('musicVolume') ??
       25.0)
     .then((savedMusicVolume) => musicVolume =
       savedMusicVolume);
   ```

4. Next, change the line that starts playing the music to the following:

   ```
   await FlameAudio.bgm.play('music/music.mp3', volume:
     (musicVolume / 100));
   ```

5. During the testing of the navigation, a bug was found where the enemies and coins were invisible when playing the game for the first time. This is due to the *z*-order priority being incorrect, which makes the map draw on top of the sprites. So, let's fix that now by setting the priority higher.

   In the same onLoad function, change the initialization of the Skeleton, like this:

   ```
   var skeleton = Skeleton(player: george, position:
     Vector2(position.x + gameScreenBounds.left,
       position.y + gameScreenBounds.top), size:
         Vector2(32.0, 64.0), speed: 20.0);
   children.changePriority(skeleton, 15);
   add(skeleton);
   ```

6. Next, update the `Zombie` initialization, like this:

```
var zombie = Zombie(player: george, position:
  Vector2(position.x + gameScreenBounds.left,
    position.y + gameScreenBounds.top), size:
      Vector2(32.0, 64.0), speed: 20.0);
children.changePriority(zombie, 15);
add(zombie);
```

7. And finally, for the sprites, update the `Coin` initialization, like this:

```
var coin = Coin(position: Vector2(posCoinX, posCoinY),
  size: Vector2(20, 20));
children.changePriority(coin, 15);
add(coin);
```

8. Now that we are done updating the navigation and music playback, let's fix one last thing.

    When George's health gets to 0, we want to trigger the navigation to show the game over screen. Open the `george.dart` file and, in the `onCollision` function, change the health check code block to the following:

```
if (health > 0) {
  health -= 25;
  hud.healthText.setHealth(health);
}

if (health == 0) {
  Navigator.pushNamedAndRemoveUntil(gameRef.buildContext
  !, "/gameover", (r) => false);
}
```

This will replace the previous `else` clause, where we had a to-do action to show the game over screen.

We have now the complete code for the game! If you run the game now, you can see the simple screens and navigate around them, and you can adjust the music volume from off to full volume.

When you have built your own game, it would be great to sell the game, and who knows – you may make the next successful blockbuster game, such as *Angry Birds*, and become very rich! In the next section, we will discuss exactly that – how to make money from your game.

Monetizing your game

Once you have developed your own game, you may want to try to make some money from the game. There are a few ways to do this, depending on the platforms you wish to support. But in this section, we will focus on the three most common ways so that you can decide what is best for you, as there are pros and cons to each way.

The three main ways to monetize your game are as follows:

- Adverts
- In-app purchases
- Purchase

In the following subsections, we will discuss each of these options.

Adverts

There are many advert providers, and each provides its own libraries for Flutter. The recommended one for mobile is Google's own Mobile Ads SDK, which Google provides an official library for. This is easy to integrate, and you will make money by showing adverts to the players within your game.

Be aware that overuse of adverts will annoy players, so please try and think of the experience the user will get while playing the game to try and balance this out.

Let's look at the pros and cons of using adverts in your game:

- *Pros*:

    a. Easy to integrate.

    b. Repeat income from a constant revenue stream.

- *Cons*:

    a. Can be annoying for users.

    b. Money paid for adverts is quite low.

Now, let's look at another monetization option, in-app purchases.

In-app purchases

In-app purchases can be a great way to make money from your game. Generally, with this type of game, you give it away free and then take small micropayments in the game, which work through Google Play or Apple's App Store.

You are purchasing virtual goods that only exist in that game. For instance, in our game, you can purchase extra lives or a better weapon to use in exchange for real money.

Be aware that some existing games that use in-app purchases have a reputation for paying to win, where the user that is willing to pay to buy the best items in the game can win the game easily. This is controversial, especially in multiplayer games where you can buy success in the game.

From our view as developers, virtual goods provide an interesting way to monetize our games. This is because the game assets are virtual, and they can be sold many times to different players and provide a reliable, repeatable revenue stream.

Let's look at the pros and cons of using in-app purchases in your game:

- *Pros*:

    a. You can sell the same virtual goods to many different users.

- *Cons*:

    a. It can be fiddly to set up in the mobile developer portals.

    b. It can be irritating to users if overused.

Now that we have discussed the pros and cons of in-app purchases, let's look at our final option, purchase.

Purchase

One-time purchases are also another valid option for monetizing your app. You can set a fixed price for your game that the users pay once.

Be aware that players tend to want to see updated content in the game, such as new levels. So, if you only make money from a fixed price, you will be maintaining the game for free, aside from any new sales you may make by updating the content.

Let's look at the pros and cons of using purchases in your game.

- *Pros*:

  a. It's hassle free, and you only have to set the price once.
- *Cons*:

  a. There's no repeat income from existing customers.

If you want to further read up on ways to monetize your game, please check out `https://flutter.dev/monetization`, which goes into more detail.

In this section, we discussed ways of monetizing your game. In the next section, we will discuss what else is worth learning to expand your game development knowledge.

What else should I learn?

Now you have mastered the basics of game development with Flame, let's look at what else you can learn that are more advanced topics but are very useful in expanding your game development knowledge.

Forge2d

A lot of games use advanced physics to make the games more realistic, such as using gravity to affect how sprites jump and fall or calculating the trajectory of a falling bird in Angry Birds.

There is a very good physics engine available called **Forge2d**, which is based on the famous Box2d engine, which is worth investigating if you want to make your games more realistic.

You can find everything you need to get started at `https://docs.flame-engine.org/1.0.0/forge2d.html`.

Nakama

Single-player games can be a lot of fun, but games go to a whole new level when you play them with your friends. Multiplayer game development is a very complex subject to do from scratch, but it is a useful subject to learn and can improve your games a lot. Fortunately, Flutter has a good library that handles all the complex stuff needed to build multiplayer games, which works well with Flame.

The library is called **Nakama**, which is discussed at `https://heroiclabs.com/docs/nakama/getting-started/`, and the Flutter library for this is at `https://github.com/obrunsmann/flutter_nakama`.

Nakama has many features. Here are a few of the things it can do:

- Multiplayer gaming between different players
- Real-time chat between players
- Leaderboards for tracking who has the highest score
- User accounts with logins

Nakama covers many more multiplayer features than we cover here, so it is recommended that you check out their website (`https://heroiclabs.com/docs/nakama/getting-started/`) for more information.

Rive

Rive is a cross-platform animation tool that allows you to export an animation and play it back, using libraries specific to each platform. If you are familiar with the old Flash animations, this is similar.

You can read more about Rive at `https://rive.app/`. The Flame library for Rive can be found at `https://pub.dev/packages/flame_rive`.

What games shall I make?

Flame is suitable for all types of 2D games, so you can make whatever game you like. The difficulty is that some types of games are more complicated to code than others.

If you plan on making role-playing games, which are very popular, be aware that these are very complicated games to make, as they often simulate real-world mechanics and require you to build a lot of content for the game.

Start simple with games such as *tic-tac-toe* and build up to games such as *Sokoban* or *Breakout*, before moving on to platform games such as *Mario*.

There is a great article at `https://gamefromscratch.com/just-starting-out-what-games-should-i-make/` to give you some more ideas about what games to make and in what order you should make them.

In the next section, we will discuss where to get help when you get stuck with Flutter/Flame.

Where to get help?

There will be times when you are making your game that you will get stuck. You may not know how to implement something or there might be a bug with the Flame library or Flutter SDK, for instance.

Here, I have compiled a list of great resources where you can seek help if you get stuck:

- **Flame Discord** (`https://discord.gg/5unKpdQD78`): Here, you can ask the Flame development team questions and get excellent advice on how to use Flame.

  We especially want to thank Spydon, Erick, and Wolfen on the Flame Discord server for all the help they gave while I worked on the book.

- **Stack Overflow**: The same people who monitor Flame Discord monitor Stack Overflow, where you can also post questions. Be sure to tag your questions with the `#flame` tag.

- **Flame documentation**: The Flame documentation can be found at `https://pub.dev/documentation/flame/latest/`, and you can find many examples and tutorials for Flame at `https://github.com/flame-engine/flame/tree/main/examples` and `https://github.com/flame-engine/awesome-flame#articles--tutorials`.

- **Flutter community page**: For more general Flutter help, please check out the Flutter community page at `https://flutter.dev/community`, where you can find links to the Flutter Discord and Slack channels.

In this section, we discussed where to get help when you get stuck with Flame or Flutter.

Summary

In this chapter, we learned how to mix our game widget with other Flutter widgets and navigate between screens to complete our game. We also gave the player the option to change the music volume on the settings screen.

We discussed options for monetizing your game and what to learn next to improve your game development knowledge. Finally, we reviewed where to get help if you get stuck with your game.

We have covered a lot in the book, and you now have the knowledge to build a variety of 2D games with Flutter and Flame. Good luck with your game development journey. I look forward to seeing the games that you create.

Questions

1. What library should we use to persist simple data such as the music volume?

2. What options are there for monetizing your game?

3. Which Flutter class is used to change screens?

4. What is the main benefit of monetizing your game with in-app purchases?

Appendix: Answers

Chapter 1

1. The minimum constant frame rate Flutter draws at is 60 frames per second.
2. The graphics engine used by Flutter is Skia.
3. Android, iPhone, Mac, Linux, Windows, and the Web can be supported with Flutter.
4. Skia is an open-source graphics engine that provides graphics APIs for drawing shapes, text, and images.
5. Dart supports both just-in-time and ahead-of-time compilation. Just-in-time compilation provides great features like stateful hot reload while debugging, and ahead-of-time compilation provides high performances when the game is released.
6. Stateful hot reload allows you to make a change to your code, reload it, and instantly see the change (it's like painting with code!).
7. Dart uses fast garbage collection for short lived objects, allowing Dart to rebuild the widget tree at 60 frames per second for smooth animation.

Chapter 2

1. `deltaTime` is the time that has elapsed between frames. This is used to ensure that the frame rate stays constant across devices with different processing powers.
2. The Flame Component System allows us to build a flexible architecture for our game which is essential as our game grows.
3. `HitboxRectangle` is used for detecting shapes that are squares or rectangles.

Chapter 3

1. A synopsis gives a high-level summary of the game's goals used to entice players to play the game.
2. George's health will reduce by 25% when an enemy attacks him.

3. George's score increases by 20 points for every gold coin collected.

4. Water is used to define boundaries that George or the enemies cannot cross.

Chapter 4

1. A sprite is a graphic or image asset that can be static or animated.

2. The functions `createAnimationByColumn` or `createAnimationByRow` return a sprite animation list.

3. `SpriteAnimationComponent` reduces the amount of extra code we need as animation is built into the component by design.

4. A range is specified using the `to` and `from` parameters to represent the start and end animation frames.

5. A base class allows us to set up common behaviors that the sprites will share.

Chapter 5

1. A HUD is a Heads-Up Display. It represents a user interface that we want to draw on top of our game, showing things like score and health.

2. To detect touches, we use the `Tappable` mixin.

3. A `TextComponent` is used to draw text on the screen.

4. A joystick has an inner control which needs to be dragged to the outer control to register a value for the joystick's direction.

Chapter 6

1. We use the `flame_audio` library to add audio to our games.

2. Loading audio into a memory cache ahead of time improves your game's performance, as we are usually going to play the same sound effects many times in the game.

3. We need to clear the buffer to prevent holding onto the resource and causing memory leaks, which may crash our game.

4. We need to listen for pause events when the game is backgrounded and resume events when the game is brought back into focus.

5. We need to store a reference to the `AudioPlayer` that is returned for longer sound effects, so we can control the sound if the game is paused or resumed.

6. We use the `volume` parameter passed to the `play` function of `FlameAudio`.

Chapter 7

1. The Tiled application allows us to create tile maps that are much larger than the physical screen of our game, by using tile sets made up of small tiles to represent things like grass or water.

2. Tile maps reuse each tile, meaning that they take up much less memory than storing a larger image.

3. Tile map data is stored in a 2D array to represent the width and height of the map.

4. We can use tile layers for representing the tiles and object layers for objects we want to draw on top of the map.

5. To adjust the map as a sprite moves around, we use a camera and set up the `followComponent` function with the component that we want to focus on while it moves.

6. We can add collidable objects as an object layer in our tile map and then create components from these by reading the object with the tile map `getObjectGroupFromLayer` function.

7. A collidable object can be active, passive, or inactive. We use these to reduce the amount of collision checks between collidable objects, which helps the game's performance.

Chapter 8

1. Web browsers require audio permissions to be enabled when first loaded to prevent web sites irritating the user with annoying noises.

2. Our game is set up with an initial size based on the dimensions of the screen. If this changes, everything now needs to be recalculated, otherwise things like the joysticks won't be positioned correctly.

3. The default `TiledComponent` doesn't need a position and size. but to fix issues when resizing, we need to be able to recalculate these values. So, we wrap the component in a `PositionComponent` to give us the position and size values.

4. We can use `canvaskit` for prioritizing performance or `html` for prioritizing download size.

5. We use the `KeyboardHandler` mixin to listen for key events.

Chapter 9

1. `lifespan` and `count` are common properties to set when using particles. They represent how long the particle should be shown for and how many should be shown, respectively.

2. Particles created a lot of objects very quickly and can use up a lot of memory, so we need to free up the memory once the particle is no longer in use.

3. `MovingParticle`, `CircleParticle`, and `ComputedParticle` are examples of particles that Flame supports.

4. Flame supports the `PreRenderedLayer` for static images and the `DynamicLayer` for animated images.

5. We need to delegate the rendering of the super class to the layer class so that the layer processor can do its work of generating the shadow image.

Chapter 10

1. We can use the `distanceTo` function to measure the distance between two position vectors.

2. The algorithm we used in Gold Rush for pathfinding is known as `A* (A Star)`.

3. We can multiply or divide the *x* or *y* position by the tile size to convert between world and grid coordinates.

4. Turning `withDiagonal` to true provides more natural movement to our characters, otherwise the characters will move at right angles which look robotic!

5. Every time we change direction, we must match the correct animation, or we will get issues like the sprite appearing to walk backwards.

Chapter 11

1. To persist simple data, we use the `shared_preferences` library.

2. To monetize a game, we can use adverts, in-app purchases, or a fixed cost purchase.

3. The `Navigator` class is used to change screens in Flutter.

4. With in-app purchases, you can resell the same digital asset to many people for a repeatable revenue stream.

Index

Hi!

I am Paul Teale, author of Building Games with Flutter. I really hope you enjoyed reading this book and found it useful for increasing your productivity and efficiency in Flutter.

It would really help me (and other potential readers!) if you could leave a review on Amazon sharing your thoughts on Building Games with Flutter here.

Go to the link below or scan the QR code to leave your review:

```
https://packt.link/r/1801816980
```

Your review will help me to understand what's worked well in this book, and what could be improved upon for future editions, so it really is appreciated.

Best Wishes,

Paul Teale

Other Books You May Enjoy

If you enjoyed this book, you may be interested in these other books by Packt:

Flutter for Beginners – Second Edition

Thomas Bailey, Alessandro Biessek

ISBN: 978-1-80056-599-9

- Explore the core concepts of the Flutter framework and how it is used for cross-platform development
- Understand the fundamentals of the Dart programming language
- Work with Flutter widgets and learn the concepts of stateful and stateless widgets
- Add animation to your app using animated widgets and advanced animations techniques
- Master the complete development lifecycle, including testing and debugging
- Investigate the app release process to both mobile stores and the web

Flutter Cookbook

Simone Alessandria, Brian Kayfitz

ISBN: 978-1-83882-338-2

- Use Dart programming to customize your Flutter applications
- Discover how to develop and think like a Dart programmer
- Leverage Firebase Machine Learning capabilities to create intelligent apps
- Create reusable architecture that can be applied to any type of app
- Use web services and persist data locally
- Debug and solve problems before users can see them
- Use asynchronous programming with Future and Stream
- Manage the app state with Streams and the BLoC pattern

Packt is searching for authors like you

If you're interested in becoming an author for Packt, please visit `authors.packtpub.com` and apply today. We have worked with thousands of developers and tech professionals, just like you, to help them share their insight with the global tech community. You can make a general application, apply for a specific hot topic that we are recruiting an author for, or submit your own idea.

Ingram Content Group UK Ltd.
Milton Keynes UK
UKHW050656250423
420716UK00003B/37